Life and Love and Why

for ordering and purchase:
www.amazon.com
www.createspace.com

"Not everyone who says to me, 'Lord, Lord,' will enter the Kingdom of heaven, but only those who do the will of my Father who is in heaven. Many will say to me on that day, 'Lord, Lord, did we not prophesy in your name and in your name drive out demons and in your name perform many miracles?' Then I will tell them plainly, 'I never knew you. Away from me, you evil doers.'"

Jesus the Christ

To Ethan, my son; may we together grow into men after God's own heart and deepen our willingness and ability to love God with all our heart, soul, mind and strength.

Acknowledgments

Thanks must first be given to God, my Lord and savior Jesus Christ.

Thank you Emily, my wife, for your listening ear as these thoughts were being born.

In addition, I want to thank Kaari Dahlman and Becca Jarvi for your advice and support through the continual forming and reforming of this book.

Thank you Ryan Bettger, Ryan Rueckert, Brendan Lorentz, Matt Hulst, Ann Solinger, Annie Beasley, Aani Rangen, Cristina Warfield, Becca Jarvi, Andrea Beagle, LeRoyce Chapmen, Dave Berggren and Jeff Zaugg for talking through these topics with me and honestly engaging in this discussion.

Thank you Mom and Dad for your continual love and encouragement. You both, in many ways, are the inspiration behind this work.

Page	Content
8	Introduction
12	Chapter 1 — The Human Problem
24	Chapter 2 — Common Assumptions
34	Chapter 3 — A Tree and its Fruit
42	Chapter 4 — Turning Inward
54	Chapter 5 — The Kingdom of Heaven
68	Chapter 6 — God is Love
80	Chapter 7 — Love and Anti-love
90	Chapter 8 — Life and Death//Love and Anti-love
100	Chapter 9 — The Face of life in Love
112	Chapter 10 — The Purpose of Pain
124	Chapter 11 — Turning Outward
138	Chapter 12 — Love's Reflection
148	Chapter 13 — The Face of Truth in Love
162	Chapter 14 — Humanity Redeemed
174	Chapter 15 — Redeeming Humanity

Appendix	Page
Confession	192
Community	193
Marriage	194
Raising Children	194
Submission to authority	196
Baptism	196
Communion	197
Reconciliation	198
Worship	198
Fasting	199
Prayer	200
Sabbath	201
Service	202
Mission	202
Evangelism	203
Giving	204

End Notes	206

introduction

There is a cross hanging on a wall inside of a church. It doesn't matter which church or which cross we are talking about; they are all pretty much the same. You have probably seen it. The cross is "pretty" with angled edges, polished wood and some are even adorned with banners, sheer fabric and ivy.

The cross is beautiful.

This, more than anything else, is the symbol of our Christianity. But beyond it being a symbol, it is also largely indicative of what our faith has become.

And it is very disturbing.

The cross to the Roman's was the overflow of their intense cruelty and demand for power. It was the most gruesome and excruciating form of punishment and death their twisted minds could come up with. During Jesus' day, outside Jerusalem's gate was a site that brought fear into all who saw it: a field of crosses, each with a body hanging from it and signs above their heads stating exactly why they were hanging there.

Don't steal under Roman rule or the cross will be your end.

Don't dishonor Caesar because you will find yourself here.

The cross was an execution steak used to manipulate the lives of those under Roman rule. It was the clearest symbol of death. No one ever survived the cross.

The cross was designed so that in order to take deep, refreshing breaths while on it, you had to push up with your legs, which were nailed at the ankles to the vertical crossbeam, so that your lungs could inflate, your diaphragm could expand and air could come in. Hanging on a cross was tiresome as the blood constantly flowing from the holes in your wrists and ankles made by the nails the Roman guards had pounded through them left you increasingly weaker and fatigued. As you lost blood, you became exhausted and many would then suffocate without the strength to push up to breathe.

If it was taking too long, the Roman guards would simply come by with a wooden mallet, strike it against your knees, break your legs and force you to stop pushing up.

The cross was always victorious. And in the process of victory, the cross became blood soaked, nail-holed, split and broken. The cross was never "pretty" and certainly not beautiful. A cross that was "pretty", free of blood and hole-free indicated that it had never been used. No one had ever died on that cross.

And yet these are the crosses we hold on to. We associate ourselves with crosses no one has ever died on. We carry a cross and adorn our churches with crosses that remain pretty, free of piercing and clean of blood.

And so goes our Christianity.

When Jesus said "If anyone would come after me, he must deny himself and take up his cross and follow me" (Matthew 16:24), he meant that you must die. Taking up a cross in Biblical context meant nothing else. There was no way around it. But for many in our context, "My cross to bear" means only a hardship to endure. We carry our cross, but they don't lead us to death.

Do we carry our crosses only when it seems convenient? Do we carry them only when the reward is greater than the sacrifice? Are our lives just riddled with Christian ritual?

God can't really expect us to carry our cross at all times, can he? That would just be exhausting.

Our crosses remain pretty.

Is it fair, or right, to assume that we can participate in Christ's resurrection without first participating in his death (Romans 6:5-12)?

I think the answer is obvious yet involves more than we have ever imagined.

This book is in part an exploration of that question and everything that comes along with it. Because the cross of Christ was the greatest revelation of love humanity has ever known, this book is also, at its core, an exploration of Love and the nuances that surround it. This is not an answer book. I am fallible. The discussion in this book is only adding to the greater conversation. It is by no means the end of it.

Life and Love and Why

chapterone.thehumanproblem
(goodnews?)

Leila's chest tightened as the sound of her father's slurred yelling filled the house. The oppressive tone of his voice felt like a boot against her throat clamping farther and farther down until it was almost impossible to breathe. Her bedroom door was shut but her father's voice overpowered all forces she used to block it. Even the pillow she stuffed against her face didn't prove to be enough. This was the second time this week she had awoken to this scene. The shattering of glass and ceramic was a sound she had become accustomed to; her mother's silence was another. Leila remembered that her father had not come home last night. This usually meant he had been out all night squandering his paycheck on rounds of drinks and at least a few lap dances.

He had always told Leila he loved her. Some of her fondest memories, albeit there weren't many, were sitting on her father's lap and falling asleep as he stroked her long dark hair. Her father then picked her up, held her against his chest and neck and carried her to her bedroom. She would often wake up in her bed the next morning still tucked in from the night before. She then would throw her pink-flowered comforter off, run down the stairs hoping to find her father to give him a big bear-hug. What she would frequently find however was a pile of cigarette butts, empty beer bottles and an otherwise empty house.

But that was a long time ago.

Her father always ran when the responsibility of being a good husband and father began to show its face. Sure, at one time he could "pretend parent" through suffering the little things like rubbing her back and brushing her hair but not when real sacrifice was to be made. When something would actually affect his desires and interests, he fled.

No notice. No warning.

He only returned when his resources ran out or when his bed seemed more comfortable than a city sidewalk or when his wife and child seemed better company than the drunks he surrounded himself with. "After all," he thought, "They at least obey the backside of my right hand." Leila's father saw all people as objects to be used for his gain and when they subverted this policy, he never hesitated to show them who was stronger. He didn't care for anyone other than himself.

He was never taught he had to.

Leila's father, Dan, had lived an interesting life. His parents had raised him under the assumption that the world would naturally teach him the lessons it needed to and therefore gave him as much independence as he desired. "Let him drink," they thought. "He will learn to dislike it and stop doing it once he wakes up vomiting, with a splitting head ache. And let him smoke. When he develops asthma or lung cancer, he will have learned that he shouldn't have made such a stupid decision in the first place."

This parenting style didn't seem to work on Dan. He already resented his parents because they had repeatedly chosen to go to casinos rather than his little league baseball games. He therefore naturally sought whatever would make him feel good in his time of pain.

At the young age of twelve he began to drink and smoke, and from this age, he essentially raised himself entirely independent of his parents except while coping with his parents' presence the few times they actually gathered for a family meal. And they didn't care what he did as long as it didn't interfere with their agenda, which was either to work or to gamble; for his father, these things often overlapped.

The lessons he was supposed to learn from his choices did not, however, form him into a person who resisted alcohol, cigarettes, or the ways of the world but rather made him dependant on them. Whenever life beat him up, it wasn't the memories of being hung over or of coughing fits that rushed into his memory but the seemingly precious comfort that came from a bottle in his hand. It seemed that the bottle was the only thing that actually treated him well, he thought; the only thing that gave him attention, care--even a sense of worth.

The day of Dan's eighteenth birthday, he punched the clock at work and walked home, as was his usual routine. But as he approached his house he noticed something different: the few belongings he had were in a pile on the lawn with a note attached to them simply saying, "Good luck with life."

Enraged, Dan kicked over his small pile of things, picked up an old baseball trophy and threw it at his parent's house. He repeated this with shoes, hockey pucks, books and rocks from the yard. He eventually collapsed to his knees and screamed at the house, "I hate you!" hoping his parents were inside to hear him.

He sat on his lawn for a few moments as he gathered his thoughts, picked up a bag of his clothes from the pile and began walking down the street leaving most of his things scattered on the lawn amongst the broken glass from the shattered windows.

This culminating experience of his life's events sent Dan down a very dark road. He couldn't keep work or relationships and within six months couldn't pay the rent, buy food, cigarettes or liquor. But Dan convinced himself he needed these things. "My only friend is the bottle," he told himself as he huddled, drunk, in an ally way trying to stay warm. "What will I do without you? Goodbye, friend," he said, tenderly to his last bottle as he threw it against the brick wall in front of him.

His dependency caused him to do things he would have never imagined himself doing. Lost and seemingly without hope, he began to steal from unlocked cars and sometimes, unlocked homes. "Those in survival mode don't have the luxury of caring for others," he told himself. He never took much; just what could be sold at pawnshops in hope that he might eat a meal that day. But this was a lie he told himself to justify his actions. The reality was that most of the money he got from the stolen goods went to bars, liquor stores, and sometimes, strip clubs.

One night while at a club, which always coupled him with alcohol, he took a liking to a particular dancer who had been particularly good to him. He waited until the morning when her shift was over and followed her out of the club and to her car. Dan had never learned self-restraint, especially when he was drunk. In fact, he had been taught that whatever he wanted, he could have it and if it was wrong, the world would teach him his lesson. Under the glow of neon lights, Dan engaged the young woman in conversation but she didn't seem to be as interested in him outside the club as she was inside. Dan, now seeing her for the manipulator she was, pushed her up against her car, overpowered her, forced her into the backseat, raped her, and to keep her silent, killed her.

Her body was never found and Dan was never charged.

His lesson was never taught.

Dan knew he had to keep a low profile and therefore relaxed his thievery and somehow, even his drinking. And over the next five years he really tried to remain in the backdrop of society. But for some reason his behavior didn't improve. It was almost as if he was now incapable of behaving differently. This was mostly played out in his relationships. Within those five years he held short but very abusive relationships with seven or eight women but they were all too strong-willed to put up with his abuse for long. That is, until he met Meg, a woman he met while working a distribution line at a factory for minimum wage.

Meg's history was unfortunately only slightly brighter than Dan's in regard to her behavior but far darker in regards to being provided self-worth.

Meg wanted someone to love her.

Dan wanted someone to manipulate.

Leila was the byproduct of this relationship.

The fact that there is a problem with humanity is evident when we look at our world. Pain, suffering, injustice and hate are all daily occurrences. When you look at the world and see the tyranny played out amongst humanity, does it seem right? Does it seem natural? Do you cringe when you hear of sex-slavery in India? Do you cry over genocide in Africa? Do you mourn for the millions suffering from starvation or lack of medicine for curable diseases? Do greed and the hoarding of money infuriate you when there are people freezing to death on city streets? Are you burdened when unfounded gossip and slander push people to suicide?

You don't have to look far to see and understand that there is a problem of evil in our world.

Life and Love and Why

In January 2003, a 19 year old man named Beau went into his father's house, took a butcher's knife from a drawer and began to walk down his street to the home of Robert Schmidt. On the way, Beau picked up his 16 year old sister and they together went up to Robert's home and knocked on the door.

But there was no answer.

Earlier that day, Beau had purchased what he thought was methamphetamine from Robert for $125 but later discovered that it was only a bag of salt. Beau had gone to Robert's home to "make things right." His intention was to cut him or to cut off one of his fingers. But when Beau arrived at Robert's house at 1:30 in the morning, Robert and his girlfriend had already taken the $125 to the casino. Instead, Beau and his little sister were greeted by Robert's girlfriend's two daughters. They knew enough not to let strangers into their home and therefore wouldn't immediately open the door. However, Beau convinced them that their mother had gotten hurt at the casino. Beau told the girls that "Robert didn't want to leave your mom alone at the casino so he asked us to come instead." The girls believed him and opened the door. When Beau and his sister discovered Robert wasn't really there, they attacked and repeatedly stabbed the two girls.

Kristyanna, the 3 year old youngest daughter died two hours later in the operating room. Her 32-pound body couldn't handle the multiple stabbings. Brittney, age 10, was stabbed 27 times. Her spinal cord was severed and although she survived the attack, she remains paralyzed from her waist down.

When questioned by police, Beau was asked how he got a cut on his hand. He said that when he was pulling the knife out of one of the girls' skull, it slipped because it was soaked in blood and it cut his hand.[i]

Ten months later, on the other side of the country, a boy by the name of Ryan sat at his computer, chatting online with a girl at school he had come to like.

Ryan, when he was younger, had not developed full language or motor skills. He therefore had to be in special education classes. When Ryan was in 5th grade, a bully started teasing him about how "stupid" he was and how bad he was at everything he did. Over the next three years, it continued and escalated to the point where they eventually got into a fist fight. Ryan was actually relieved because he "got a few good punches in before it was broken up." But something odd happened after the fight: the bully befriended Ryan.

They started talking regularly online and as trust grew, Ryan divulged more and more information about himself and started joking around with his newfound friend. Ryan's new friend, the old bully, finally got something more sinister he could use to torment Ryan and started telling everyone at school that Ryan was gay. Over the next 6 months Ryan fought off these rumors but with little avail. Ryan, in hopes to squash the rumors approached one of the most popular girls from his school online one night and started a "relationship" with her. They talked often and the girl said many times that she liked him too.

When Ryan went back to school in the fall to start his eighth grade year, he approached his new girlfriend for the first time in person.

He was never prepared for what would happen.

In front of her friends she told him he was just a loser and that she didn't want anything to do with him. She said she was only joking on-line. He later found out that she and her friends thought it would be funny to make him think she liked him and to get him to say a lot of personal, embarrassing stuff. In fact, she had copied and pasted their private instant message exchanges into ones with her friends.

One month later, Ryan committed suicide.[ii]

Does this break your heart?

Is this really how life was intended to be lived?

There is something wrong with the human condition. If it were not the case, my heart would not break over children stabbing each other over drug money. I would not be concerned for women who are addicted to drugs by men who force them into sex trafficking. My heart wouldn't drop when seeing news reports on suicide bombings that kill hundreds of people. I wouldn't turn away from seeing reports of parents who beat their children to death. I wouldn't be concerned when I learn that 25 thousand children die every day from hunger related issues.

Why does my heart break?

Does yours?

If concern hints of "goodness," it seems there is something good within every one of us, something that is naturally concerned for the welfare of at least one other outside ourselves in addition to our own survival.

Hitler, after all, even loved a woman.

Part of the solution in solving the problem is drawing the good out and understanding what or who the implicit good is. But for many this problem is a cognitive trap to understanding that there could actually be a loving God. The problem of evil is for many the great hang-up in believing in God. This will be discussed in more detail below but for now I want to focus on the source of the problem (which I will say here that I confidently believe is *not* God).

I am going to assume then that you have rightly understood sin to be the problem behind the evil in our world. To simply say "sin is the problem" however leaves us with a rather ambiguous dilemma. How do you understand the problem?

Contemporary notions of sin (mainly the evil we do) have largely overlooked the biblical implications and severity of its doctrine. It is assumed in our relativistic, post-modern and subjective context that the love of God will triumph over all sin in the end and we will all therefore walk confidently into the throne room of God with our sinful nature intact, expecting the love of God to usher us in to our own personal glory. This is what popular scholars in our modern day have coined the "God-of-appeasement" theory, which implicitly denies the actualization of sin in the world. After all, God loves us so much. Do you really think he would send someone to hell?

The God of appeasement promotes a "meet you where you are at" mentality of the Christian faith or a "come as you are" approach to discipleship. I do not deny the validity of these claims; what I do deny are the implied messages behind these claims. It is true that God loves us with the full extent of his being, but it is also true that we can deny God's love through the way we live our lives (Jonah 2:8). The more appropriate question then is not "Does God love me?" but rather "Do I love God" (John 14:21)? God's love for all of humanity is an accurate theological and biblical principle (Lamentations 3:22; John 3:16; Romans 5:8—to name a few). We as humans may not always "experience" this but it does not negate it as fact. As C.S. Lewis said, "You must have a capacity to receive, or even omnipotence can't give."[iii] Or in other words, if we do not love ourselves, then we have no frame of reference in which to place God's love for us because to love yourself means that you acknowledge you are loved. So without the love of self, we tend to shove God's love off as a concept that only the select blessed few can comprehend. "Look at the world," we say, "Do you really believe there is a loving God?"

Yes, I do and he is calling us to himself.

So, while to "come as you are" is appropriate, the Bible no where states that it is acceptable to remain where you are.

Not only do modern definitions of sin fail to settle the ambiguous problem of sin when set against a biblical understanding of its doctrine, they also—and especially—remain uninformative when considering the severity and role of sin in ones life. We must remember that our notion of sin and our claim to salvation are inextricably linked; how one understands sin will naturally affect how one understands their salvation. Therefore, when our understanding of sin remains confusing, so does our understanding of salvation.

Most contemporary Christians understand a contemporary definition of sin but assume their purely cognitive belief in Jesus Christ assures them of their salvation. And considering this is what most people seek through their Christianity, they are content with their understanding—or rather—their confusion.

If people's salvation was taken away, would they seek more earnestly to live a more authentic Christian life? Or is it actually the case that the majority of Western Christianity simply doesn't care and they put themselves into the Christian mold because it is what is most readily available and offers them the greatest reward (implicitly) for the least amount of work?

It seems our modern gospel is hollow and lacks real transformation: it lacks the real Christ. We are therefore in desperate need of "good news"—of a real gospel.

The difficulty lies in the fact that most people's definition of "gospel"— and therefore their salvation—is solely attached to the death and resurrection of Christ. The "good news" was that we were saved because of what Christ did through his death and resurrection. To merely "believe" that Jesus "died for our sins" seemingly releases us from the burden of living a life aligned with Jesus' life. If our Christian focus is to believe only in the death and resurrection of Jesus as our ticket to freedom and heaven, why focus on his life or his instructions? Doesn't his death and resurrection assure us of eternal life? Isn't good news already mine?

Eternal life is indeed good news but Jesus, even at the start of his ministry, claims "The Kingdom of God has come near. Repent and believe the *good news*" (Mark 1:15). In Luke, Jesus begins his ministry by quoting Isaiah: "The Spirit of the Lord is on me, because he has appointed me to proclaim *good news* to the poor..." (Luke 4:18). Simeon, upon seeing Jesus as an infant, proclaims "My eyes have seen your salvation" (Luke 2:30). This seems odd considering the salvific moment is usually characterized as Jesus' death, not his infancy.

The gospel, according to Jesus, was not tied solely to his death but primarily to his proclamation and existence including his birth, life, death and resurrection. Salvation is tied up in the entirety of who Jesus was. The problem is that the gospel is rarely discussed holistically. We tend to sever Jesus' life from his death and claim that the latter has a higher priority for believers than the former.

The difficulty for modern Christians lies in that we cognitively accept belief in the cross of Christ but not in his life. We cuddle up next to the cross and lash out against those who threaten it. In so doing this, however, we actively divorce ourselves from Jesus' life and teachings; not to mention the rest of the Bible, especially the Old Testament. We cling to his cross rather than take up our own; we say, "Jesus loves me and this is enough!" but forget that Jesus said if we loved him, we would obey him (John 14:23). Obedience to Jesus assumes that we know what he commanded but for many people, even that exploration is asking too much of them.

We want the grace of God but for the least amount of cost. But as Mother Theresa has asked, is grace, or faith or love that doesn't cost anything, worth anything? I would agree with her conclusion that it is not.

Dietrich Bonhoeffer also understood this. He states,

> Grace is represented as the Church's inexhaustible treasury, from which she showers blessings with generous hands, without asking questions or fixing limits. Grace without price; grace without cost! The essence of grace, we suppose, is that the account has been paid in advance; and, because it has been paid, everything can be had for nothing. Since the cost was infinite, the possibilities of using and spending it are infinite. What would grace be if it were not cheap?[iv]

I hope it would be real and transformative. But why seek costly grace when what we are searching for is available for far less? Why pursue costly grace when we are told we can obtain "The *free* gift of eternal life through the God who loves us so much that he sent his Son to die for us?"

All we have to do is ask him into our heart, right?

One might think that God's great love would assume cheap grace as a viable option for salvation. But it is not.

Before the Gospel can be good news, it must first be bad news. The bad news is that we are all terrible sinners in desperate need of good news. And while understanding our own sin and depravity is important, the point is not to merely receive the good news and continue on with our lives but to be transformed into good news for all people. Good news therefore requires much of us. Jesus did not simply come to die and rise from the dead. While our salvation does not exist without their happening, Jesus' life and ministry also invite us to participate in his salvific work. Salvation is not merely handed to us—it too requires something of us for if following Jesus is anything, it is sacrifice.

Love does not exist without it.

Our problem is that we have been programmed to believe that salvation is in the death of Christ and we therefore largely neglect his life. We are afraid to venture into what Christ called his people to live like because it asks of us more than we are willing to give. If we are taught we can keep our salvation through our ignorance, what is our motivation for learning?

But what if we can't keep our salvation through ignorance? What if our salvation is a façade? What if what we thought we were clinging too doesn't actually exist for us? Would this motivate us to change and enter into a greater and deeper journey? Or is it the case that we actually prefer death to life?

It seems Adam and Eve did.

Our motivation for change must be equally matched by a proper understanding of what we ought to be changed into. Without it, we merely change directions but have not provided ourselves traction to begin progress.

If it is therefore true that we must first understand what we are being saved from in order to understand salvation, a holistic understanding of sin must be acquired...

chaptertwo.commonassumptions
(sin)

If it is true that we must first understand what we are being saved from in order to understand salvation, a holistic understanding of sin must be acquired.

"Get up! Do you realize it is already noon and you are still in bed wasting away your Saturday?" Andy couldn't believe he lived in this mess. Dirty clothes hung over the window to block the light from bothering his roommates sleep; books were strewn across the floor with little concern for their sell-back price; puddles of beer sat on his desk from last night's party and the room had a taste that seemed like a mixture of ashtray and garbage can.

This was not how he imagined his first year of college.

"I'm not only tired, I'm hung over, so let me be." Andy's roommate, Mark, covered his head with his pillow. The muffled light streaming through the dirty clothes was evidently too bright for him.

"I have a chemistry final on Monday, and I need to study. And I thought you said you were going to stop drinking," Andy said as he pulled the clothes from the window revealing a faint mist of smoke still hanging in the air.

"It helps me de-stress from a long week. And what does it matter? It's not like I'm hurting anyone. Everyone does it, so it's not like it makes me a bad person."

"So you are going to wait until you kill someone while driving drunk before you claim that your drinking habits are wrong," retorted Andy as he wiped up the beer that had spilt next to his computer. "And besides, I don't do it. If drinking is the standard for being good, I must be really-good!"

"Seriously? I think your cynicism takes you off of that list. Drinking is not wrong or bad. It can't be. Doesn't your church hand out wine and crackers on Sunday morning?"

"Are you really minimizing the Eucharist to a wine tasting party?" Andy said as he shook his head in disgust by the very idea.

"All I am saying is that if the church does it, it can't be wrong. They set the standard, right? Don't they make the rules? Don't' they write the lists of what is right and wrong? They can't contradict themselves, can they?

Drinking has to be permitted." Mark was now making his way down the ladder along his lofted bed. He jumped from the third rung and landed directly in front of Andy.

"Your logic is mesmerizing," Andy joked as he shoved Mark's dirty clothes into Mark's chest. *"And you stink worse than this room does."*

"If the church wanted drinking to be wrong, they wouldn't promote it themselves. This is all I am saying. And besides, even if it is wrong, isn't that why the church created confessional booths?"

"You're an idiot," Andy annoyingly remarked as he moved two half-empty beer bottles off of his chemistry book, picked it up and began to study. *"You better hope to whatever god you believe in that your goodness will be good enough and that that's really what it's all about; but if you keep making these kind of comments, I personally doubt it will be the case. But showering might help!"*

We have already determined that there is a problem with humanity. What we came to conclude, however, was that we don't really have a good idea of what that problem is and because our salvation is tied to being saved from this problem, we have a rather misunderstood and ambiguous idea of salvation.

The goal of the next two chapters is to hopefully shed some light on the problem so that later we can begin to understand what Christ is really calling his redeemed and saved people into.

Most people view sin in one of four ways: as a list, as a fall, as an effect, or as a chasm. Some view it as a combination of the four.

Sin as a list

In C.S. Lewis' book, *The Pilgrim's Regress,* the main character, John, is confronted with the rules of the land, something he was previously unaware of:

...The Steward then took down from a peg a big card with small print all over it, and said, 'Here is a list of all the things the Landlord says you must not do. You'd better look at it.' So John took the card: but half the rules seemed to forbid things he had never heard of, and the other half forbade things he was doing every day and could not imagine not doing: and the number of the rules was so enormous that he felt he could never remember them all. 'I hope,' said the Steward, 'that you have not already broken any of the rules?'...'because, you know, if you did break any of them and the Landlord got to know of it, do you know what he'd do to you?' No, sir,' said John: and the Steward's eyes seemed to be twinkling dreadfully through the holes of the mask. 'He'd take you and shut you up for ever and ever in a black hole full of snakes and scorpions as large as lobsters—forever and ever. And besides that, he is such a kind, good man, so very, very kind, that I am sure you would never want to displease him...'[v]

The vast majority of people see our dilemma this way: sins are those things that we are *forbidden to do*. And most people will also probably tell you that "the list" is comprised of everything that is fun in our world.

Consider the idea of the seven deadly sins: wrath, pride, lust, envy, greed, sloth and gluttony. We surmise that if we can stay away from these behaviors, all is well and our Christian existence is being lived appropriately. But don't forget, recently a few new sins were added to the old: drug dealing, having excessive wealth, polluting the environment, genetic manipulation and a few others all make up the list of sins the "good Christians" will stay away from.

In this light, our relationship with God is largely contractual. We are obligated to follow certain parameters in order to keep God happy and therefore stay in right relationship with him. After all, God "is such a kind, good man, so very, very kind that we would never want to displease him." But consider the implications:

1) This idea requires an exhaustive list of "don'ts" in order for it to be valid. But who has the authority to make such a list? Many believe the Bible is the source of this list as it is the authoritative word of God. Because this is the case, the Bible too becomes very legalistic and contractual.

2) When we attempt to live in accordance with the list we become legalistic and pharisaic in our approach to life. Therefore we become exceptionally judgmental of those who cannot abide by the rules of appropriate living.

3) We assume God cannot be serious in his high expectations and attempt to live as close to the standards as we can. Furthermore, we don't really believe God could be as merciless as this penal theory of sin suggests. Therefore, we are left with a bunch of "Christians" who show up to church and do "Christian" things but who don't have a relationship with God. Church becomes a social network (at best) with no trace of genuine community.

4) We quickly realize this list is impossible to follow on any given day and end up abandoning the list and therefore abandoning God and possibly become very cynical of God and religion all together. Or we realize we have failed on any number of points on the list and give up hope for redemption all together. "If I am already damned," some say, "what is the point in trying at all?"

5) We begin to believe that bad things happen to us because of our inability to abide by the list. Or, we believe the opposite, that material wealth and "blessings" will be given us if we simply follow the rules on the list.

What this understanding has done is create "Christians" who show up to church looking to be blessed because they feel they have accomplished all God has asked of them. They want their reward for their faithful living and when it is not handed them, they become angry at God for "He," they say, "Is the one not meeting his end of the bargain."

Sin as a fall

This theory implies that we somehow look up at God from our imperfection and therefore need correction and improvement to retain his good graces. We often use the language of a "Fallen humanity" but it is never actually used biblically in relation to the first sin. It is indicated within editorial comments but not the original text. Did humanity "fall", as if they tripped by accident, in relation from God or did something else metaphysical (though with clear physical implications) happen? Again, there are negative implications to this belief:

1) Our focus is set on improving ourselves and ridding ourselves of "sin" in hope we might "rise" from the "fall" into proper relationship with God.

2) Our religion then becomes inherently works based focusing on what we do rather than who we are.

We then become entirely guilt ridden when on any given day we fail to check off all our spiritual boxes. We begin to compare ourselves to the really good Christians and wish we could only be like them but we at least find assurance that we aren't like the really bad people. Christianity exists on a sliding scale and a very slippery slope.

Sin as an effect

Developed more recently from post-modernism, this theory defines sin as those behaviors which have an immediate negative effect towards me or towards another individual. For example, consensual, premarital sex ought to be viewed as sin only if a negative outcome ensues. With proper protection, some say, this will rarely occur and therefore this behavior is not sinful in nature. As for the guilt involved in premarital sex, one might say that after the first time there could be feelings of guilt and shame but not after the fifth or the tenth. If the conscience no longer condemns, than it must not be a sin. There are negative implications here as well:

1) We believe effect assumes immediacy. We therefore live our lives under the assumption that if nothing bad is happening to me, I am in the clear.

2) The ethical and moral code become our own experiences and therefore we become the judge of what is right or wrong as we watch the world play out before our eyes.

What we fail to understand however is that the reach of our choices are beyond anyone's comprehension. It assumes that we can physically see the effect of every choice we make. But we cannot. What we do may not be painful or hurtful in the moment or to a physical body but is it possible that in ten years, we may reap the effects of our past sowings (Galatians 6:7) or that someone was once hurt by what we did or said and simply did not communicate it?

Sin as a chasm

Probably the most popular way of viewing sin (especially within evangelical circles) is known as "*the chasm.*"

You have probably seen it:

This idea basically states that the nature of sin is primarily a divide between humanity and God: sin separates us from God. If you are familiar with the illustration, you will know how the divide is "crossed" — quite literally with the cross of Christ:

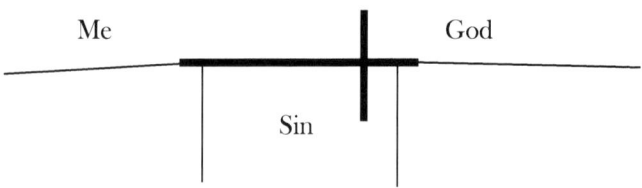

This imagery seems to make a lot of sense when first looking at it. Take a moment to look at the imagery. Ask yourself four questions in accordance with these images:

1) Prior to the cross, what is *my* relationship to God?
2) What is *my* relationship to sin?
3) How is sin conquered?

4) What does this image implicitly tell me about the nature of sin?

According to this model, prior to Jesus, no one had a relationship with God: the divide of sin did not allow for it. Furthermore, sin is entirely outside of the self. Sin is something we must overcome, climb out of or surpass but I have no connection to sin other than to simply cross over it in order to enter into God's presence. To do so, God was gracious enough to provide me a bridge and I simply have to attest to believing the bridge actually exists and then I can find "salvation." Again, negative implications are evident:

1) While this model does promote God and Jesus as a great savior—and indeed it is so—it passively removes our responsibility to live a godly life. There is no participation in the cross. Nothing is required of me.

2) It completely neglects the need for repentance and encourages a fully nominal view of Christianity (You were in need of crossing the divide; God provided you the means to do it through the cross of Jesus thus you are saved!). By consequence, it focuses one-hundred percent on the death of Christ and neglects his teaching and life as necessary to right relationship with God and therefore salvation.

3) This model promotes that we as humanity have been completely cut off from God. The relationship between humanity and God is a severed one: prior to Christ, according to this model, we can only assume humanity had no relationship to God.

4) It therefore promotes a very deistic worldview apart from Christ: God is the creator—the divine watchmaker, if you will—who sits enthroned above the earth and simply watches it tick.

What we are left with is a God who doesn't actually care about us. He is not personal. Christ is, but not God. Those without Christ, including those prior to Christ, are left completely without hope. But this isn't the case for God interacted personally with humanity prior to Christ; and even now he intimately interacts with those who have not accepted Christ (something that will be discussed in more detail later).

Now it is true that sin causes separation from God (Is. 59:2). But if we consider that God is Holy (literally, "set apart"), to say we are separated from God simply means we are no longer bound to Him, not that there is a literal divide between us.

For most of you, my well-Christianized readers, you probably understand the intention of the model: Christ redeems us from our sin. But for people who first encounter Christianity from this model—because they received it on a tract on a street corner or saw it in a bathroom stall, or it was left for them as a tip at the restaurant they work at—the implications of misunderstanding this model are potentially destructive.

All of our models have proven to be flawed on their most fundamental level. *The list* promotes half-hearted faith in Christ. *The fall* makes Christianity a works based religion. *An effect* assumes we are the source behind determining what is good and what is evil. And *the chasm* promotes passive Christianity.

In order to understand the nature of sin holistically and to construct a more appropriate model, I believe we need to understand its beginnings. And this is a story we will unpack throughout the rest of this book...

chapterthree.atreeanditsfruit
(sinnature)

In order to understand the nature of sin holistically and to construct a more appropriate model, I believe we need to understand its beginnings. And this is a story we will unpack throughout the rest of this book...

Genesis 2 and 3 describes a time when humanity walked side by side with God. The relationship they shared was one of humanity in submission to God: "You are free to eat from any tree in the garden; but you must not eat from the tree of the knowledge of good and evil, for when you eat of it you will surely die" (Genesis 2:16-17). Understanding their role as created beings, they worked the creation and lived in faithful relationship with God and with one another. It was only when they were exposed to the lie that they could "be like God" (Genesis 3:5) did they move forward with eating the fruit.

C.S. Lewis puts it this way:

> What Satan put into the heads of our remote ancestors was the idea that they could 'be like gods'—could set up on their own as if they had created themselves—be their own masters—invent some sort of happiness for themselves outside God, apart from God.[vi]

They who once rightly understood their place as creatures now set themselves up as creators. After their sin, they were side by side with God vying for control, kingship, creative capacity, priority and reign. They became self-centered rather than other centered seeking *personal reign* and benefit with every circumstance and interaction.

Sin, then, is a Kingdom concept and must be understood within a kingdom context.

Prior to the choice to disobey God, God was enthroned in the lives of Adam and Eve: He was their God. However, they willfully dethroned him and by their lust for power, enthroned themselves as choice-maker and ruler of their lives (Gen. 3:1-7). They had become obedient only to themselves.

They became their own kings.

Therefore, Adam and Eve, in their own willingness, established for themselves personal kingdoms in contention with God's and with one another's:

> "...the Lord God called to the man, 'Where are you?'

He answered, 'I heard you in the garden, and I was afraid because I was naked; so I hid.'

And he said, 'Who told you that you were naked? Have you eaten from the tree that I commanded you not to eat from?"

The man said, '*The Woman you put here with me--she gave me some fruit from the tree, and I ate it.*'

Then the Lord God said to the woman, 'What is this you have done?'

The woman said, '*The serpent deceived me, and I ate...*" (Genesis 3:10-13).

As it can be seen, Adam and Eve continually deflected the responsibility of their choice to the next in line in an effort to protect themselves. By blaming Eve, Adam exerted his rule and power over her in lifting himself above her and therefore suppressing her. Eve, in turn did the same with the serpent. Furthermore, by choosing to sin in the first place, both assume God's role as the caretaker and king of their lives.

There was thus a metaphysical change in their being from God-lovers to self-lovers (John 14:24) and this act continues to permeate throughout humanity. By creating a full-predisposition towards the self rather than God, Adam and Eve brought condemnation to all people through their own trespasses. Thus we were all made sinners because of the initial disobedience to God (Rom. 5:18-19).

Unlike God, however, Adam and Eve, being creations, did not have the capacity to rule adequately. Thus, we, as humans, have the nature of sin within us. We must therefore ask how this initial decision to sin impacts the overall nature of sin.

What Adam and Eve hoped to attain by their choices was *personal reign* rather than *communal submission*. The nature of the sin they committed was one of selfishness: they set themselves up as the one who reigns over other people and over God.

Martin Luther states that the nature of sin is *Homo incurvatus in se*: humans bent in on themselves. Sin, in other words, is thoroughly a problem of reign. We as sinners are bent in on ourselves seeking our own good prior to the good of others.

To most people this is not shocking or radical theology. Self-centeredness, pride and judgment (over others) have often been characterized as the foundational sins. Our need to "surrender" too has been a cornerstone for Christian growth.

This then leads to a popular theological debate: that certain sins are inherently worse than others. However, when we realize that sin is a problem of the self-centered heart rather than a hierarchy of do's and don'ts, all of those actions we call "sin" are now realized as only different manifestations of our own selfishness and desire to reign over others.

In other words, *there is only one sin we ever commit.*

Stop for a moment and think about this and its implications.

Everything we call sin are simply different forms of our reign over another person.

There is only one sin that is ever committed. You don't commit numerous sins. No one does. You simply commit the one sin in many different ways. Everything we call sin are simply different forms of our reign over another person. The way you commit this sin may look different than the person across the hall, or the person in prison or the pastor at your church, but the sin is the same. We all exert our reign over others: we all are human. We have set up a self-kingdom alongside God's kingdom and we have declared war.

We say that murder is a terrible sin (and indeed it is) but justify our lying as of little consequence, concern or significance. It's not as bad as taking a life, is it? It's not hurting anyone, is it? In the kingdom understanding of sin, however, both murdering and lying are forms of my reign and superiority being exerted over another person. Could it actually be the case that me being angry with my brother or sister is the same as murdering them? Could it actually be the case that me lusting after a woman is the same as committing adultery (Matthew 5:21-30)?

Granted, the consequences might not be the same but the sin is, and therefore both are deserving of death. Anger and murder, lust and adultery, each are only a different manifestation of my personal reign and rule.

This is in part why Paul encouraged the Philippian church to "do nothing out of selfish ambition or vain conceit, but in humility consider others better than yourselves" (Phil. 2:3). Paul understood the Christ follower as one who was marked by a complete abandonment of selfish interest and sought to fulfill the needs of others above their own as a response to the great love of God proven through Jesus Christ.

Thus, this understanding of sin—that sin is really our attempt to reign in God's place—informs us why previous models of sin fail in regard to allowing transformative growth to develop from their premises.

Sin as a list

This model suggested that sin is a list of moral "thou shalt nots" that are primarily laid out in the Bible. This model naturally lends itself to a hierarchy of sins and also the necessity of an exhaustive list for it to be valid. Thus, humanity finds itself squirmishing over what it does (the individual sins) rather than what it is (a race of people bent towards their own good). When sin is recognized as a matter of reign rather than a matter of don'ts, however, we begin to understand that a meta-sin overlaps all sin. Consequently, understanding the correct nature of sin equips us to fight our battle at the level it needs to be fought: holistically. If our battle is merely with the list rather than with the core of who we are, transformation is futile.

For many readers of the Bible, the list of do's and don'ts finds its place in the Levitical Law. Many therefore stray away from reading the Old Testament law because they believe its supposed legalism comes from a wrathful God. However, if one understands that the overall principle of the Old Testament Law is to express Love for God and others (Deuteronomy 6:4-5; Matthew 22:40), this legalist view falls flat. Love is to inform us of how we live our lives, not to squash under a list of do's and don'ts.

Sin as a fall

Likewise, the idea that we *fell* or somehow became imperfect creatures when the original sin happened assumes that we need perfecting or improvement. "If I could somehow stop committing some particular sin in my life," we say, "My Christian faith would be improved." Once again, our goal is focused on the individual acts of sin rather than the sin nature.

Although this may be true to an extent—that we're always meant to be growing more like Christ—simply working at the cessation of the acts of sin in my life becomes ineffectual. The moment I succeed in overcoming one sin, I must look to the next one on the list and seek to overcome it. But what happens when I stumble, when the sin reveals that it wasn't actually defeated? The process must start all over. The argument becomes cyclical. I constantly find myself back where I started.

Moreover, who decides which activities or thoughts are sinful and which are not? I mean, I don't smoke, drink or have affairs. What other sins are there? This model suggests that the only sins worth fighting are those that the church society deems as inappropriate.

Today, the so-called Christian majority is greatly concerned with homosexuality and adultery but often turn their backs to gossip, greed, envy and passivity. We are told not to worry about gossip or greed for these are characteristics of our culture, *including* the culture of the church. The church decides what is right and what is wrong, and what it does is naturally right (they're the "Christ followers" after all). "Good" Christians follow the church party line. If the church is greedy, shouldn't we suppose that greed is appropriate? If the church gossips, shouldn't we be allowed to do the same?

The model has superseded Christ's likeness.

This type of Christian existence fails to correlate the symptoms with the disease. When we conceptualize our mission as one correcting our imperfections, it is as if we are taking cough drops to cure bronchitis. It may help to reduce our coughing but the disease is still destroying us. When our aim is the reduction of our sin rather than the correcting of our nature, transformation cannot take place.

We are not in need of improvement but of surrender. Once we surrender, improvement will take care of itself. Our problem is not with the expressions of our wickedness but with where these expressions are born from: the problem is with our nature. When the nature is corrected, so then will its expressions.

Sin as an effect

This theory is probably the quintessential scapegoat theory of sin. It promotes the habit of justification, lying and cheating. We assume that if nothing negative is born from my behavior, I must be living a good life. We therefore go to great lengths to protect ourselves and those around us from experiencing the ensuing effects of our decisions.

But again, who determines what a negative effect is? To me, a sinner bent towards self-reign, "negative effect" harms only me and those I am close with. The decisions I make that harm those whom I don't know don't concern me. This mentality however only promotes what the previous two theories of sin have: the reducing of my negative effects on others will somehow make me a better Christian.

This is simply not the case, nor is it the point.

Sin as a chasm

The bridge or *chasm* motif of sin too suggests that the problem of sin is something outside of the human person and that its goal is our own salvation. The imagery suggests that as long as cognitive assertion is placed in the cross, the cross exists to conquer our sin. Christ achieved this for us (since we could not) and therefore we are saved.

But if salvation remains in the cognitive, salvation does not exist. Our new goal becomes not salvation but ardent belief, and demonstrating it through a Christian lifestyle. Therefore, the Christian existence develops into a works-based religion: I do what I do because in so doing it will achieve a goal. Christ becomes the means to our own personal glory rather than the goal himself.

Notice too how the issue in question is the sin rather than the sinner (reign). The goal is to overcome the sin as characterized by those actions I do outside of myself rather than to confront the sinful nature inside me. We quickly fall into the same trap that the other models promote: I will merely focus on the cognitive belief in Jesus to avoid my sins. This model, like the others, negates the need to actually *do* anything with the sin in one's life; it merely evades the issue by focusing on the redemptive work of Jesus on the cross.

No where does it ask anything of *us*. Not even repentance.

And yet Jesus' first message is one of repentance: "repent for the Kingdom of God is near..." (Matthew 4:17). Repentance was at the center of Jesus' teachings, and the Kingdom of God cannot be divorced from it.

While I understand that these are mere models and thus cannot explain the entirety of the human problem in a few cute little diagrams, it does not negate the fact that incorrect assumptions and implications are constantly drawn from them.

Hopefully by the discussion thus far, we can begin to understand how transformation might take place and how the kingdom of God might be advanced first by a correct understanding of the nature of sin. If nothing else, I pray that in reading this, your eyes will be opened to the truth about the nature of sin, and that it will help you to recognize those times when you prioritize yourself over others.

But simple recognition will do you no good.

Something greater must still be done; still be learned.

chapterfour.turninginward
(goodness)

Something greater must still be done; still be learned.

"Do you really think that my goodness won't be good enough to get me into heaven?" Mark asked, interrupting Andy from his studying, as he came back from the shower.

"Is that all you want?"

"What?"

"To get into heaven?"

"Well, yea. I don't want to end up in Hell and be poked by demons with pitch forks all day." Mark had now put his shirt on which ironically had the outline of a demonic looking figure, bent over with a pitch fork in its hand with the words "Hell Yea" in red letters across the chest.

"So what are you doing about it?" Andy never once looked up from his text book but continued to jot down notes as their conversation continued.

"I don't know. Nothing intentional I suppose. I'm just a good person so I think that should cover my bases. I mean, the murderers, thieves and lawyers have something to worry about, but not me. What have I ever done that would be deserving of hell?"

"Don't know. You did cut in front of that elderly woman at the grocery store last week."

"She was taking forever! Seriously, how long does it take to pick out a pack of gum? I certainly cannot be judged for that! Plus, I made up for that when I stopped completely at the stop sign on the way home."

"Wow, you deserve a badge of honor. Have you ever thought that maybe what is required of you is not to be good but to be great?" Andy still hadn't moved his gaze from his chemistry text book.

"Great?!" Mark thought the idea was absurd. "Who even determines that? No, goodness is the standard; everyone knows that." Mark was now sifting through a pile of dirty jeans. He picked up a couple to smell them and noticed most of them were stained from beer spills and pizza sauce. *"I really should get one of the girls down the hall to do my laundry."*

Andy, for the first time turned to look at Mark and immediately noticed his t-shirt. He shook his head in disbelief and disgust. *"Are you really that lazy? How can you, of all people, even have a definition of "goodness?" This is a perfect example of my point. Who determines what is good or great and who determines the standard? Your idea of "greatness" and mine are completely different. This is obvious to anyone who has ever seen us in the same room. So what does this tell you about the nature of goodness? I mean, you have already admitted that you judge your being good against murderers and lawyers. Doesn't that tell you something? What about the pope? Or Gandhi? Are you good compared to them?"*

"Well, probably not." Mark thought for a minute to himself, *"But they're great people, and if what is required of me is to be good, then I must be alright."*

"Have you listened or understood a single thing I just said?" Andy couldn't believe how shallow Mark's thinking was and ran out of patience. Andy couldn't wait to get out of there, out of this living situation and back home in a week once his finals were over. *"You do know you are an idiot, right?"*

"Ah, but I am a good idiot."

"Please leave," pleaded Andy as he turned back to his studying.

Thus far, we have attempted to show that we lack a holistic understanding of sin and because this is the case, we are left with a rather shallow understanding of not only our salvation but also what Christ is asking of those who claim his name. In the previous chapter, we examined how the nature of sin is really a nature, a disposition rather than just an action, and therefore there is only one sin that any of us ever commit. Hopefully, this realization has already supported you in your battle against the sin nature. But please know that it is a *lifelong* battle, and that you will only participate in victory when God releases the final call for the new heaven and the new earth (Revelation 21-22).

Our contemporary Christianity, however, has taught us to battle the *expression* of our nature rather than the nature itself. Unfortunately, this has led to the promotion of a compartmentalized Christianity: I will fight the sins that our churches deem as inappropriate but I will neglect to struggle through the "small" stuff such as gossiping or impatience—those sins that our Christian sub-cultures by in large ignore.

One of the main difficulties with our previous notions of sin is that they do not promote how sinful we actually are. When our focus is on the expression of sin, we can confidently declare that we are good Christians if we restrain from drinking excessively, smoking, sex outside of a marital relationship (sex is of course defined by intercourse so anything shy of that is typically accepted), swearing, cheating on bigger, more public projects and extensive lying.

But this is no longer the case. Nor is it the point.

When we begin to understand that our dilemma is a matter of our reign over and against God manifested through our actions (both seen and unseen), we begin to see not only how all-encompassing the problem of sin is, but also what lies at the root of all sin:

We are incredibly selfish people.

If I were to juxtapose my life with the list of inappropriate, sinful behaviors as typically promoted by our Christian sub-cultures, I would discover that I am a very good person! I don't drink, smoke, swear, have affairs, look at pornography and I don't even have road rage; plus, I really try not to gossip or think poorly of others. I am the Christian poster-boy.

But sin is not just about my external behaviors or my internal thoughts. Sin deals with the way I view myself in comparison to everyone around me, including my own self-conception.

With this understanding, now every interaction and thought I have, whether intentional or simply in passing has the potential to be a sin-filled interaction. Sin is now a relational concept. If sin is relational, then the potential for sin exists within every interaction I have whether this interaction takes place in the physical or the mental world.

Notice too how worthless grace and mercy are when I view sin as merely my bad actions. We make God's love, grace and mercy comparative constructs and because we see ourselves as good people, we don't have a desperate need for them and therefore there is no desperation for God because what he offers us doesn't really seem that important. The Christian poster-child who has it all together does not understand the value or need of God's love or forgiveness. What is there to be forgiven from when my sin is not really that bad? If I claim to be without sin, then there is nothing to confess and repent of and therefore nothing to be forgiven of (1 John 1:8). I don't really need God; he is more of an added comfort, the security blanket that insulates me from the evil world.

It is only when I grasp that sin is a relational in-dwelling facet of my being that I begin to experience the insurmountable value of grace, mercy, love and forgiveness, because I realize that sin invades so many of my thoughts and actions. I—yes—me, the "good" Christian, am in desperate need of grace, mercy, love and forgiveness simply because I am truly a terrible sinner.

What I find odd is that in my own life, my reign over others is seen not primarily in the way I view myself but in the way I view others (albeit there are many who overtly view themselves as superior to others). I don't often go around thinking "I am better than you," but I do unfortunately think about how flawed you are or what about you annoys me or that the attention you receive should be mine. My reign is implied by the way I view you. In every put-down or suppression of another person is the equal but opposite exaltation of the self; and conversely in every thought of superiority of the self is the equal but opposite suppression of another person.

And I am not the only one who thinks this way, nor am I the first. The roots of this problem reach all the way through human history to its very foundation.

Let us again consider for a moment what actually happened in the Garden of Eden when Adam and Eve chose to eat of the fruit.

In the beginning, Adam and Eve shared the presence of God: worked alongside him (Genesis 2:15), openly conversed with him (Genesis 2:23) and walked with him (Genesis 3:8). They, in other words, shared God's presence. Considering that in the Hebrew language "presence" and "face" are the same words, one could also say that they "looked into the face of God." Essentially, this means that their natural disposition was directed towards the triune God who exists within a reciprocal love relationship (the constant giving and receiving of love). The fact that they were initially created within and directed towards this type of relationship will become exceptionally important later once I have laid some ground work. But here, for the sake of simplicity, Adam and Eve's pre-sin relationship to God looked something like this:

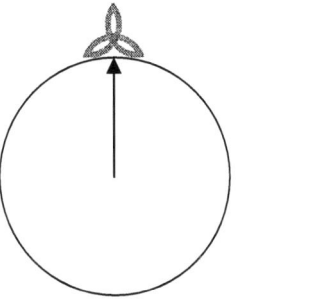

Adam and Eve's lives and souls were directed towards their reciprocal love relationship with God and also with one another. One cool morning however, a serpent came along and asked Adam and Eve if God was serious in his description of what would happen if they were to eat of a certain tree. They both responded with an emphatic "yes." The serpent however was very crafty and after thinking to himself for a moment said, "Death!? No, God did not mean that you would die but that your eyes would actually be opened and in so doing, you would be like God" (Genesis 3:5)!

Adam and Eve then looked at each other, glanced over to the tree and noticed that it was beautiful, not evil. Plus it offered the additional benefit of gaining wisdom. They thought, "The tree cannot be all bad. Surely God desires us to be wise."

And so they ate of the tree God had forbade them not to.

And immediately they felt the burden of the weight of disobedience. I can only assume it felt like the weight of six feet of dirt upon them. No, it was probably more like tearing the soul from the body, for they had died.

All of our models for sin essentially attempt to make sense of this one moment in human history. Most have thought that what took place was a divide or separation between humanity and God as has already been discussed.

I want to suggest that something far simpler happened: they turned around. The human disposition shifted from a reciprocal love relationship with God to self-love. Their love was now bent inward. They became self-serving and self-reigning. They turned their backs on the face of God, his presence and relationship with him:

Adam and Eve's choice for self-reign unfortunately had lasting consequences that are still affecting every child born into our world. Our nature is no longer oriented toward love of God manifested in love for one another, but is wholly directed towards seeking first to satisfy the wants and needs of the self. We have taken upon the burden, and unfortunately the death, of our first parents.

This is simply because humanity is born from one seed. Paul wrote to the Roman church in hopes that they would understand the universal problem of sin that all people are in: both Jews and non-Jews (Romans 3:23). He writes, "Just as sin entered the world through one man, and death through sin, and in this way death came to all people, because all sinned..." (5:12). Humanity, according to Paul's understanding, all derive from a single source: Adam. Considering this is the case, all of humanity is born from a single creator. If both the problem and the creator are universal, then not only is the need for redemption universal but also for all of humanity to share the same pattern of redemption: Christ the creator God. Christ is for all and his redemption is for all and the redemptive process is through him alone.

This process begins with submission—not analysis. We can sit and think of how we have failed as Christians all day long but until we understand our place as a subject of a king other than ourselves, we will never grow to rule over the sin in our lives. Rather we will continue to be ruled by it. For sin is always crouching at our door; it desires to have us but we must rule over it (Genesis 4:7).

Everything in our life, including our nature, tells us that we need to conquer the dilemma on our own. Anything else would assume humility and this idea is entirely at odds with our natural human tendency toward self-reign.

Do you see the irony?

We naturally recognize the sins in our life and their destructive power, and therefore seek to cure ourselves. We run towards being "good" and doing the "right things." We desire a merit based existence because then we control our own destiny. But this also assumes that we are the judge behind determining what is good and evil. Goodness, in other words, becomes a relativistic concept. We say to ourselves, "I don't murder, rob others, have affairs or cheat. I am a good person." If my own conscience exclaims "I am good" in comparison to "the bad guys" in my society, why should I worry?

But do you see what has happened? Our concept of what it means to be good has become completely external in nature. Our "goodness" is wrapped up in the behavior we perform as judged by the world's standards, just as our concept of sin is. Sin becomes antithetical to goodness, and since goodness is relativistic, so then is sin. We tell ourselves that as long as my goodness remains in tact as compared to the truly evil people around me, I am in the clear.

But our relationship with God is not based on our being good. If it was, we might as well follow a different God. By making "goodness" our goal, we are in fact worshiping not the God of Christ but a reflection of our own attempt to be God. If our goal is to be good, we are living out of a works-based religion, which is not the message of Christ.

Unfortunately, though, it is what Christianity has largely become.

This is the case primarily because we promote that the goal of Christianity is to attain heaven or "salvation" someday. Our "relationship" with Jesus therefore is a means to an end, namely our personal salvation.

But notice where this leads us.

If our goal in following Christ is our own personal salvation, or generically heaven, then it is entirely selfish in nature. The expressions of our Christianity have simply become different manifestations of the sin in our lives.

In this regard, Christianity becomes like every other world religion. Every world religion has two foundations. The first is that they are works based (that my merit will achieve for me what I desire) and the second is that they are fatalistic (that their goal rests after this life). Sadly, the ones who are called to be salt and light to a pagan religious world are really no different than the followers of those pagan religions: we too are fatally goal oriented through good works.

A good friend of mine once spent a month in Thailand and came back with some incredible stories regarding her time in this primarily Buddhist country. There was one story in particular that I found to be very interesting. She spoke of her visit to a Buddhist temple which just so happened to be shaped like a stereotypical Buddha. As she approached this giant, bald and placid facsimile, she immediately noticed the enormous amount of stairs she was going to have to climb to get inside it.

Life and Love and Why

And to her dismay upon reaching the temple, she realized it was entirely hollow.

Literally, this giant Buddha was empty.

She spent half her morning walking up its stairs, but upon achieving her goal, she saw all her toil was worthless; this Buddha could offer her nothing.

Similarly, when we devote ourselves to good works in order to "achieve" salvation, we spend our whole lives trying to attain vague promises of glory. And when we finally climb that last stair, there is no reward for all our hard-won good deeds.

We receive an empty Buddha.

The fact of the matter is that the burden of merit is more than anyone can honestly bear. Striving solely after merit puts us in the seat of God, declaring that we can do it on our own and that somehow, without the help of anyone else, we can achieve that which we desire. But we were never created with the capacity to achieve anything. We were never meant to play the part of God.

In addition to our inability, merit based faiths ironically make us doubters of our ability to do good. They constantly prompt their followers to look over their shoulders wondering if their work is enough. But who determines how much good is good enough to appease the gods? At what point does the scale tip in our favor? We are not provided the parameters by which merit is judged, and therefore we enter back into the cycle of relativistic good in comparison to our fellow humans. But we were never meant to be judges of what is good and what is evil.

Thus we find ourselves trying to attain on our own, within our own fallen human nature, what only divinity can accomplish. As C.S. Lewis said,

> In setting up a good life as our final goal, we have missed the very point of our existence. Morality is a mountain we cannot climb by our own efforts; and if we could we should only perish in the ice and unbreathable air of the summit, lacking those wings in which the rest

of the journey needs to be accomplished. For it is *from* there that the real ascent begins. The ropes and axes are 'done away' and the rest is a matter of flying.[vii]

We are all seeking the divine but it is foolish to think that it can be found by human efforts. Flying is not a gift naturally given to humanity. There must then be some other means by which we are to attain this ability.

But an ability assumes too much of us—it gives us too much credit. It is more like attaining a realization. We must realize that we have no ability within our own efforts. This is the starting point for Christian growth.

Another friend of mine who has spent significant time in Buddhist culture told me of a discussion he had with a Buddhist monk. One day in conversation with my friend, this monk came to the conclusion that his selfless actions, though he did them so he could eventually escape the cycle of life and death (samsara or reincarnation), were inherently selfish. "What good are selfless actions," he said, "If in the end we do them so that we will receive a reward?" Isn't selflessness in this regard just another form of selfishness?

Within our Christian subcultures we too typically set our mind on attaining the heaven at the end of life. But notice how this ambition is entirely self-serving. Most people are "Christian" because they would rather end up in heaven than hell someday. Again, Jesus is the means to an end, and this end revolves entirely around us. We too are entirely fatalistic: our goal is in the future—post this life.

Somewhere along the way we developed an understanding that eternal life begins when we die. We forget that if the soul is eternal and it is within us, then even now we are preparing to live forever.

To the apostles, eternal life began when the Spirit of God dwelt within believers. When the Spirit of God descended upon a new believer, that person was brought out of eternal death to which they were naturally enslaved. According to the New Testament, then, in our natural state we are eternally dead. It is only when we are born into a different nature, the Spirit nature, that we are brought alive. After all, Jesus said, "I have come to give you abundant life" (John 10:10). Ought we not to assume then that we were dead prior to him invading our world?

Jesus seems to think so.

But this isn't the way we have been programmed to think. We have been told that salvation, eternal life and heaven are things we will acquire sometime at the end of time. But our goal is not to work to assure that our end will be a favorable one through our good works. The whole idea of good works assumes you are only partially invested in your spirituality.

Salvation and heaven cannot be won. They can only be given.

And then accepted.

And if salvation is given by accepting grace (Ephesians 2:8), it means having a capacity to hold it but when our hands are full of our own piety and good works, there is simply no room.

chapterfive.theKingdomofheaven
(love)

And if salvation is gained by accepting grace (Ephesians 2:8), it means having a capacity to hold it but when our hands are full of our own piety and good works, there is simply no room.

"And now we go to the state penitentiary where Angela has the latest from the execution of Dan Jackson." Leila couldn't believe what she was watching. She had secretly prayed for this day to come many times in the last fifteen years but now that it was here, she wasn't sure she could bear it.

Angela's descriptions brought Leila to tears. "Dan Jackson has been convicted of the murder of Jennifer Smith whose body was found when some hikers discovered a clear plastic tarp which appeared to be full of bones protruding from a ledge along the river after some very heavy rains had washed away the bank. Her leather boots, the only article of clothing still intact had traces of blood on them, which lead police detectives to Dan Jackson, a frequent patron of the club Jennifer worked at. He was arrested on the charges of first-degree murder..."

Leila had always wondered where the seven, half-inch scars on her father's face came from. She now knew. Jennifer had clawed at his face when she was being beaten down and raped.

"...The execution is set to take place by lethal injection at 2:30 this afternoon. Dan had requested a news conference last night so that he could apologize publicly to the family he had hurt but as the time came for him to speak, he was unable to say anything. Psychiatrists say he went into a state of delusion most likely because he was looking death in the face. He only muttered what sounded like fearful expressions of his impending death. All that could be understood was "not hell, please, not hell.""

Leila couldn't stand to hear anymore and shut the television off. She sat alone in her apartment remembering the immense physical and emotional abuse her father had put her through, not to mention her mother. "That felt so much like hell," she thought as she ran her hands through her hair. "Will his afterlife be any different? Is the afterlife only retribution for all we have done here? Do we all only get what we deserve?"

Leila opened her eyes to reach across her coffee table and picked up a frame which held a picture of her daughter. "How then will my afterlife be any different?"

We have thought all along that salvation, heaven and eternal life began only when we died.

We imagine ourselves standing before beautiful, elaborate white pearled gates as St. Peter ushers us into paradise. We picture ourselves on top of white, fluffy clouds wearing white gowns playing harps with the angels and we all have halos around our heads. I am not sure why or how this image developed into the ideal for what an eternal state would be but somehow it persists.

When I was young my concept of heaven allowed me to walk through walls and on water. I played baseball all day long and ate Mexican food for every meal. There was no need to sleep because no one ever got tired and no one ever aged. I am not sure why some people were old in heaven while others were young. It would seem odd that I would have my youth while others were not allowed this opportunity and had to contend with bad hips, walkers and canes. I suppose that maybe if I were older when I had this vision, I too would have the heavenly age at which I dreamt.

But do you see how this vision catered to my fancy? Heaven was something I created for myself and everything I did there was self-serving. It was literally my amusement park by which all people there served me in whatever ways I could imagine. Who wouldn't want to go to a place like this?

It is simply unfortunate that this place does not exist. This is in part because heaven is not this other-worldly, fleeting realm that the "good" humans escape to upon death. If you remember from the last chapter, the afterlife is not this thing that exists or is initiated upon death but an existence that has already begun.

Heaven is better described as the *new created order* (Revelation 21:5) rather than the escapist picture we have often attributed to it. Heaven is not "out there" but exists here and will exist here as a restored and renewed earth. Revelation gives us a picture not of humanity escaping the world to go to God but of God and heaven coming to earth: "I saw the

Holy City, the new Jerusalem, coming down out of heaven from God, prepared as a bride beautifully dressed for her husband. And I heard a loud voice from the throne saying, 'Look! God's dwelling place is among the people, and he will dwell with them'" (Revelation 21:2-3). In the end, it is earth that is recreated as our final dwelling place, not the clouds of some imaginary paradise.

What Jesus did, in part, through his resurrection from the dead was begin the process of restoration that will find its fruition upon his return. He is the alpha and the omega, the beginning and the end. He is the first instance of the new creation and he is also its fulfillment. A new humanity has been born: that which was old has been made new; that which was dead has been awoken.

Redemption has happened. The new creation has begun and humanity has been reborn. It is our charge now to enter into the new humanity and assist in the continuing redemption and making new of humanity and the earth.

If heaven is a new creation and this new creation started with Christ's defeat of death through his resurrection, then heaven has infiltrated our world. What we have now is simply a taste of what is yet to come.

Revelation describes that when the heavens and earth are fully restored, those who are here will "see his face" or if you remember, we could say, "Share his presence" (Revelation 22:4). Together we will reign alongside God (Revelation 22:5). We will eat of the tree of life (Revelation 2:7; 22:2, 24), an option given to Adam and Eve (Genesis 2:9, 16) but one they denied in favor of the forbidden one. But when we partake in this tree, we shall live forever in the restored creation. In other words, Eden will be restored and with it our initial humanity and intended relationship with God.

We are merely standing on the fringes of heaven still shackled to the grave which we just crawled out of.

We have been programmed to think, however, that heaven and eternal life begin only when we die. We are therefore extremely interested in the end times, developing outlines and timelines of what will take place in those days, as well as paint graphic descriptions of what it will be like for those who suffer through Armageddon as we who have been Raptured look down in disgust from our thrones above on those terrible, terrible sinners below.

But is it best to assume that the study of the end times (eschatology) is only a study of the future? The apostles believed that all of the time post Christ's defeat of death was "the last hour" or the final days (I John 2:18; II Peter 3:3). In other words, we are still in the "end times." If this is the case, then the end is now and still yet to come: it is inaugurated but not yet fulfilled. With his resurrection from the dead, Jesus broke history from its then-current trajectory and established a new course heading for the new kingdom which he inhabited.

The presence of God encountered in Jesus Christ translates the expectant future hope of redemption and restoration into a present reality. World history has met its single intended climax in Jesus Christ. John 5:24 states, "I tell you the truth, whoever hears my word and believes him who sent me has eternal life and will not be condemned; he has crossed over from death to life." Life is not gained nor is God's kingdom established only as a future hope, but is found as we encounter the presence of God in Jesus Christ (John 18:36).

Eternal life is a present possession.

Many might say that if heaven has infiltrated earth, heaven is not a place I want to end up someday. In looking at the current evil state of the world, how can this be heaven? The problem is though the old king of this world, the serpent, has been defeated through Christ's resurrection, he is in no hurry to give up his reign. We therefore live today in the tension of a territory ruled by two kings: God and Satan. Thus, we see the beauty of what will be only as a "reflection as in a mirror; then we shall see face to face. Now I know in part; then I shall know fully, even as I am fully known" (I Corinthians 13:12).

All of our current models of eschatology attempt to make sense of how God will, in the end, finally put this opposing king to rest. The futureness of our present theologies never allow us to entertain the possibility that we already live in the "end times," and have been since Jesus' resurrection. Eschatology is better defined then as the study of God's reign rather than a study of the end simply because this allows us to acknowledge the "end" as the now.

But we like the idea of a future heaven because it allows us the comfort of thinking that in our turmoil, suffering and pain that we will someday escape it all and be repaid for all the afflictions we have endured. Because we have endured so much, we feel like we are owed a greater existence and therefore place our hope in an end that will provide it.

Notice again how highly we think of ourselves.

Rest assured, God will be vindicated and all evil and sin defeated. Peter, who wrote to encourage his readers through intense persecution both physically and spiritually, gives us a clear vision of what this day will be like:

> Above all, you must understand that in the last days scoffers will come, scoffing and following their own evil desires. They will say, 'where is this coming he promised? Ever since our ancestors died, everything goes on as it has since the beginning of creation.' But they deliberately forget that long ago by God's word the heavens came into being and the earth was formed out of water and by water. By these waters also the world of that time was deluged and destroyed. By the same word the present heavens and earth are reserved for fire, being kept for the Day of Judgment and destruction of the ungodly...but the day of the Lord will come like a thief. The heavens will disappear with a roar; the elements will be destroyed by fire, and the earth and everything done in it will be laid bare (II Peter 3:3-10).

The description is not provided solely to give us an account of what the end times will look like but rather to incite his readers to live appropriately before God. Peter continues by saying,

> Since everything will be destroyed in this way, what kind of people ought you to be? You ought to live holy and godly lives as you look forward to the day of God and speed it's coming...so then, dear friends, since you are looking forward to this, make every effort to be

found spotless, blameless and at peace with him. Bear in mind that our Lord's patience means salvation (II Peter 3:11-15).

Peter therefore only writes concerning the future to inform his readers of how they ought to live in the now!

This was precisely the point of all the talk regarding the "day of the Lord" in so many of the prophetic texts of the Old Testament. The proclamation of this day was meant to spur the people of Israel into repentance. They thought that simply because they were Israel, the chosen people of God, this would keep them safe in their times of idolatry. The prophets warned them that this would not be the case. Salvation, redemption and vindication were reserved for those who were covenantally faithful through repentance; not for those who were nationally the people of Israel (Amos 5:18-27; Zephaniah 3:6-17; Malachi 3:16-4:6).

Our study of the end, then, cannot merely be a cognitive exercise but must inform us and spur us on into thinking of how our journey towards Christ is either succeeding or failing now. Or in other words, because the end deals with the fulfillment of God's reign and because the end has already started, we must ask ourselves out of whose kingdom are we living?

That of God's?

Or that of my own?

If you remember our initial discussion on the nature of sin, we discussed how sin is most appropriately spoken about within kingdom/reign language. Sin occurs whenever my reign is exerted in thought, word and deed over and against another person. It is the action of my superiority at the expense of those around me.

The nature of reign is such that we give allegiance to whomever we deem as worthy of our rule. Do I desire to surrender to my will and therefore my wants at whatever cost? It would seem this is the trend our western culture is promoting. And why not? It only seems natural. But when we submit to our own reign we naturally become the judge of what is good and what is evil and what typically ends up being good for me ends up being evil for someone else. When I take, someone else has to give.

This is the intricate dance our culture is trapped in: the promotion of individualism at the expense of others.

Notice how the promotion of the self puts us in a battle ground with all other people. It is a realm where we are always looking over our shoulder making sure we aren't being stabbed in the back or that we haven't been already.

So, at the foundation of every sin is our own desire to reign over others. Some might say that, generically, it is selfishness. Therefore, some again might say, an appropriate response to sin is to be selfless or unselfish. Thus, what becomes godly, just and within Christian circles, "The kingdom of God" are hospitable, humanitarian, and philanthropic activities. This is the current promotion of "the social gospel" or a gospel that is primarily concerned with issues of justice, oppression and the poor. The fight to alleviate these injustices is a clear biblical principle. The difficulty however lies with the promotion of societal-centered justice at the expense of theocentric or God-centered justice.

What often occurs is that we place our search for justice above our search for God and so our search for justice has become void of God. The social gospel has become for many mere philanthropy and rather than justice being an overflow of the Spirit of God in us, we have made it an idol.

I do not deny the importance of our search for justice and liberation for the oppressed or philanthropy for the benefit of humanity in general. But the fulfillment of the social gospel (i.e. the end of injustice) will not bring about the cessation of sin and therefore usher in God's reign. And this is the harsh reality: where God does not reign, sin does. There are only two kingdoms, that of Satan's-which promotes we are the ones who should reign—and that of God's.

We cannot inhabit both. We cannot serve two masters.

And we would be foolish to think Satan does not recognize this, for he is "craftier than all the other creatures" (Genesis 3:1). One of his greatest tricks has been to mask service toward him with seemingly devoted service toward God.

Philanthropy is great; but if it is void of God, it is done in the service of Satan.

Consider again the insights of C.S. Lewis:

> If you asked twenty good men today what they thought the highest of the virtues, nineteen of them would reply, Unselfishness. But if you had asked almost any of the great Christians of old, he would have replied, Love. You see what has happened? A negative term has been substituted for a positive, and this is more than philological importance. The negative idea of Unselfishness carries with it the suggestion not primarily of securing good things for others, but of going without them for ourselves, as if our abstinence and not their happiness was the important point.[viii]

Do you see how unselfishness or selflessness is at its core still the promotion of the self? The focus is far too often on what I am giving up rather than how you are gaining or the focus is on how I will be celebrated for my selflessness. Our motivation for selflessness, more often than not, is that we hope to receive honor and glory for our great deeds. But as our Buddhist friend realized, if the attention, focus and motivation are on what I will gain from my activity, how is it selfless? It is merely the façade of selflessness undergirded by self-reign. Even the "Wicked Witch of the West" understood this:

> *One question haunts and hurts*
> *Too much, too much to mention:*
> *Was I really seeking good*
> *Or just seeking attention?*
> *Is that all good deeds are*
> *When looked at with an ice-cold eye?*
> *If that's all good deeds are*
> *Maybe that's the reason why*
> *No good deed goes unpunished*

Life and Love and Why

(*No Good Deed, Wicked*)

"Good deeds" are punished not because God is sadistic but because too often than not they are void of true goodness and righteousness. This does not mean that we should not do them. Jesus said that we are to give generously of what we have but to make sure we do not condemn ourselves in the meantime. We are to give of ourselves for justice and mercy, but to take care not to "strain out a gnat but swallow a camel" (Matthew 23:23-24). In other words, when our good acts are done for selfish ambitions, we are worse off in the end than we were when we began.

If our actions were truly selfless, they wouldn't be called such; they would be called "love." In this one word (and everything that comes along with it) is packed the entire meaning of life.

No wait. I am sorry, the meaning of life is not found in *that* word and concept because in our western culture, simple love is far too pathetic a thing to hold that much weight.

Think about it.

What ideas does the word "love" draw to your mind? Maybe it's infatuation. We are *in love* when we experience the "fluttery butterfly feeling" in the pit of our stomach when that special someone walks into the room. Or maybe it's the idea of sex, since "making love" refers to that activity. Perhaps it's as simple as Valentine's Day and everything that is associated with it: hearts, cupids, the colors red and pink, chocolate and roses. Maybe your best friend comes to mind or the image of a mother holding her baby. Or maybe it's Mexican food, a certain type of car, a movie you recently saw or a paint color.

I personally love the Minnesota Twins but I also love my wife. I love my son, my best friend and I love God.

But can I, or better yet, should I love the Twins in the same way I love God? Do I love my best friend the same way I love my wife?

Life and Love and Why

Our language does a great disservice to love and unfortunately by consequence to our Christian existence. I say "I love God" and "I love the Twins" in the same breath. I understand that I don't mean the same thing, but the world around me does not. What is even more unfortunate is that the expression of my love for the Twins is often more dedicated and exuberant than the expression of my love for God. Our actions rarely reflect that we love God in a different type of way than we love our sporting events.

So can the purpose of our existence really rest on such a confusing concept?

It can through an understanding of what the concept of love means on biblical terms. By understanding the Greek language and the Jewish notion of love, perhaps we can come to a new definition of love that will support us in realizing how it is the defeat of personal reign.

Love in Greek is a robust and multifaceted term. In fact, because of this, it exists in four forms: phileo; storge; eros; and agape. Unfortunately, the English language condenses all four of these terms into a single word with multiple nuances. In doing so, we English speakers lose the original unambiguous meaning when we read the Bible, and as a result, the biblical principle being taught is grossly skewed.

Phileo. This word is only used a handful of times in the New Testament. This type of love is the love I have for a dear friend. It is a charitable and consistent love: I *phileo* my friend Jeff. Consider the city name of *Philadelphia* or the word *philosophy*. Philadelphia is a conjunction of two Greek words: *phileo* (love) and *adelphos* (brother). Hence, "city of *brotherly love.*" Philosophy is also a conjunction of two Greek words: *phileo* (love) and *sophia* (wisdom): the *love of wisdom*, or wisdom that is cherished.

Storge. This term is not used in the New Testament. This is the love a parent has for a child — particularly the mother. It is the love of affection. It too is one of consistent affection. Recognize, however, that there is a difference between the love a mother has for her child and the love she has for her good friend.

Eros. This word is not used in the New Testament but holds significant meaning in the Greek language. We get our word *erotic* from this Greek word for love. This is appropriate considering that *eros* signifies sexual desire for another person. This is the love of passion; it is the love of "lovers." It is this love that produces butterflies in your stomach when a certain person walks into the room. It is also the most transient of all the loves. In sum, *eros* is the promotion of promiscuity, sex, infidelity, the risqué and lust.

This is the primary definition of love our western society promotes. One cannot watch a half hour of prime time television without being inundated with expressions of this type of love. Not only in our entertainment and advertisements, but it is frequently also the subject of voyeuristic news. For example, recently two individuals were arrested for being "caught" having sex in a public restroom with a crowd of people around them cheering them on.[ix] We live in a sexualized society. Is it any wonder that sex sells? It is the one definition that directly appeals to the senses and imagination. Because we live in a capitalist society, sex is an important part of our economic stability and therefore our culture.

And I would argue, as many probably would, that sex is easier than love.

But in our culture, it seems sex *is* love. If we really understood love, however, we would realize that our sex is more often than not void of love; or at least void of agape which we will quickly come to realize is the most important of them all.

Agape. Ninety-nine percent of the time "love" is used in the New Testament, it is referring to this type of love. Agape is the love of self-sacrifice, service and is wholly other-oriented. It is enduring and long-suffering: it is fully committed to its task at whatever cost. It seeks not the benefit of the self but only the benefit of the other. Consider 1 Corinthians 13:1-4:

Agape is patient, *agape* is kind. It does not envy, it does not boast, it is not proud. It is not rude, it is not self-seeking, it is not easily angered, it keeps no record of wrongs. *Agape* does not delight in evil but rejoices with the truth. It always protects, always trusts, always hopes, always perseveres.

Agape never fails...

Agape is the giving of oneself for the betterment of another. It is wholly committed to the dying of the self so that another might experience life.

In Judaic thought, the four are woven together, because *agape* is what forms the basis of all other types of love. *Phileo* that is absent of agape is not friendship—it is isolation. *Storge* that is absent of agape is not parenting—it is tyranny. *Eros* that is absent of agape is not love—it is lust.

Agape is the essence of God. And therefore where agape is absent, so is God, his presence and Kingdom.

Where *agape* is absent, sin reigns.

And so we find our meaning and existence not in our western notion of "love" but in the notion of agape. Understanding sin as my reign over others allows us to see how *agape* defeats sin. Agape is the expression of giving back my reign to God. An agape type of love is the defeat of my own interest and reign for it is the only activity in our world that is wholly other oriented and seeks only the benefit of the other with no concern for the self.

Agape is the Kingdom of God manifested in our world.

Agape is the expression of heaven realized now.

Life and Love and Why

chapter six. God is love (covenant love)

Agape is the Kingdom of God manifested in our world.

Agape is the expression of heaven realized now.

Andy was in distress.

Because his need was so great he thought that a probable solution to this need would be a great god. He had not been to church since college and therefore asked himself where he might seek out such a god and came to the conclusion that the church on the corner—the building he had driven past every day for the past three years—would be a viable solution or if nothing else, a good start.

One beautiful spring day, he, together with his daughter, walked to the large stone structure and began the ascent up the many freshly swept, cobble-stoned stairs. The journey had its own sense of glory as if this ascent took them up the very stairs of heaven. The stairs were lined with perfectly pruned bushes and flower beds that seemed designed to welcome a king. Icons were etched in the stained glass upon the church building as if the saints themselves were welcoming them into the very presence of God.

When Andy and his daughter reached the pinnacle of the stairs they noticed that their climb had led them to what appeared to be the entrance to the Garden of Eden. Upon the wooden door was carved a beautiful mosaic or an artist's vision of the first utopia. A man and a woman stood naked yet unashamed and they were both happy—even joyful. Lions were lying with lambs, mice with cats, sharks and fish swam side by side; creation was at peace. The presence of God was depicted as three strands of light swooping through and over the entirety of the door. At the center of the left door was a single tree full of leaves but with its leaves falling to the ground below. On the right door was a similar tree, different only in that its leaves remained alive and attached.

Both had yet to be eaten from. Both were beautiful.

After gazing intently at the door, Andy thought to himself, "The love of God must dwell in this place." The door gave off an aura of glory such that one would think to even touch it would be a sin. Tempted, and still in distress, Andy raised his hand and struck the majestic door.

But there was no answer. And so he struck the door again.

After standing there for what seemed to be an eternity, watching his hopes for appeal and release begin to vanish, he took his daughter's hand and began the descent back down the stairs, back into despair.

But then, hope.

The door creaked open and behind it stood an older man wearing a black robe. He said nothing. Andy, still holding his Daughter's hand, turned and slowly mounted the steps to the door, took a breath, and began to speak:

"I know you don't know me; I am a stranger to you and have never been to your church, but I am in desperate need. I recently lost my job and I can no longer afford to feed or clothe myself or my daughter. I am sick and my insurance was lost with my job and I cannot afford the medicine I need. Is there anything you or someone else could do to help? Anything at all?

The response was long in coming.

"Do you take me as a fool?" said the man in the black robe as he stared intently at Andy, never once making eye contact with the girl. "You are a bum manipulating this innocent child in hopes that I would extend pity. You are nothing but a drunk looking for money to buy booze. It would be foolish of me to waste the congregations sacrificial giving in offerings on such an obvious ploy. Don't you know this is the house of God? It is therefore a place for the righteous, not for the sinner."

And with that, the utopic door boomed shut and Andy, with his daughter beside him, faced once more beautiful artistry of a door depicting that the love of God dwelt here.

The most direct expression of who God is in the entire Bible is that he is love (I John 4:8, 16). Please recognize however that love is not God. God defines love; love does not define God. That would put love as our god rather than his personhood, Jesus Christ. All of John's writings—his gospel and his letters—are peppered with the idea that God dwells in those who follow after him. Because this is the case, the most obvious expression of who the disciples of Christ are is *agape* love.

Jesus affirms this time and time again: "A new command I give you: love one another. As I have loved you, so you must love one another. By this everyone will know that you are my disciples, if you love one another" (John 13:35).

It is this section of scripture—and many others like it—that prompted Peter Scholtes to write a hymn some forty years ago entitled "They'll Know We are Christians by Our Love:"

> *We are one in the Spirit, we are one in the Lord*
> *And we pray that all unity may one day be restored*
> *We will work with each other, we will work side by side*
> *And we'll guard each one's dignity and save each one's pride*
> *We will walk with each other, we will walk hand in hand*
> *And together we'll spread the news that God is in our land*
> *And they'll know we are Christians by our love, by our love*
> *They will know we are Christians by our love.*

And the sentiment is true.

Why, then, are Christians today so despised?

If love is our standard, could it be that very few Christians actually exist?

There was once a day in human history when Christians were hated because of their love. Their radical love for one another and for God spat in the face of the polytheistic, emperor-worshiping culture, a cultural focused on individual power and personal gain. Today however Christians are known more for their judgmental, hypocritical, narrow-minded, anti-gay, anti-abortion, and "we are against so and so..." stances than they are for their love of one another or of God.

Is it any wonder why most Christians are looked on with disdain?

The problem is that we acknowledge God's reign and demonstrate our love for him through ritualism. I will partake in the sacraments, go to church, do my devotions, pray regularly, put "Jesus fish" on my car and wear a cross necklace, and by these activities and decisions, people will know I am a good Christian. What we don't often realize is that by participating only in these rituals we lay the foundation for a compartmentalized faith. Jesus is simply the structure built on to the side of my life—he doesn't infiltrate the whole thing.

And please don't tell me that he should. Who wants that burden?

We like ritualism because it is naturally meritorious, which therefore gratifies our sinful nature. We desire to be seen for the great work *we* are doing. But Jesus has a lot to say about those who strive after ritual instead of shifting their nature back towards agape love for one another. He says things like,

> "...[Y]ou hypocrites! You travel over land and sea to win a single convert, and then you make that convert twice as much a child of hell as you are. [...]You clean the outside of the cup and dish, but inside they are full of greed and self-indulgence. [...]You are like white-washed tombs, which look beautiful on the outside but on the inside are full of the bones of the dead and everything unclean. [...]You appear to people as righteous but on the inside you are full of hypocrisy and wickedness. [...]How will you escape being condemned to hell?" (Matthew 23:15, 25, 27-28, 33).

Well, if you remember, hell too is in part a present reality. Hell exists wherever God's reign does not. Considering that the foundation of God's reign is agape-love marked by self-sacrifice that benefits others, the escape from hell comes with the shifting of our nature back from self-reign to God-reign. Our only hope is to redirect our lives to God in love for him and for one another (Matthew 22:39).

In other words, it's all about love. And it always has been.

What we sometimes run into in our reading of the Bible is that we tend to detach it from the human hands that wrote it. We somehow believe that it fell from the sky and thereby divorce it from its original languages, cultures and settings. We say "It speaks to all people at all times" when in reality it directly speaks to certain people in a particular time in history.

Of course, the Bible has much to say to me but only if I understand what it first said to its original readers. Otherwise we just end up proof texting God's word to make it say whatever we want it to. This has been the source of much atrocity in the name of God over the years. Biblical interpretation is hard but it is a necessary task for faith, clarity, life and love.

The lack of good Biblical interpretation has brought many to this strange idea that the God of the Old Testament was somehow different than the God of the New. That the God of the Old Testament is seemingly focused on law, wrath and judgment, while the God of the New Testament is focused on grace, love and mercy. Somehow, God's interaction with his people is different depending on which Testament you are reading.

But this is simply not the case.

Love has, since the beginning of time, been the focus of God's interaction with his people. Many people stay away from reading certain portions of the Old Testament because they think it is all law and legalism. While it is true that there are portions that seem like long lists of rules, we must understand that underlying these rules is a purpose to increase the Israelites capacity to love more fully. God set up standards not legalistically, ritualistically, or for his own benefit, but because by living out this love-based lifestyle, his people would experience the best possible life attainable. The law was "The Idiots Guide to Life, Love, Holiness, and the Presence of God."

The guidelines established were part of God's *hesed*—his covenant love for his people. God did not establish a contract based on legalism with his people but a covenant based on grace. He desired a covenant so that his people would know what love is and what love is not. The basis of this covenant was known as the shema, which in Hebrew, means "hear":

> Hear O Israel, the Lord our God, the Lord is one. Love the Lord your God with all your heart and with all your soul and with all your strength (Deuteronomy 6:4-5).

This passage is the principle the Israelites were to live by. All the other commandments are simply commentary on this one instruction. The Ten Commandments, for example, were provided to give basic instruction on how to love God (the first four) and love others (the last six). The other 602 commandments are also practical instructions on how to love your neighbor and love yourself. While on the surface these look like "thou shalt nots," the underlying principle behind every instruction given was a matter of love for God and love for others.

The difficulty is that, for the Jews of the Old Testament, the law presumably became the source of life, instead of love. If this were not the case, legalism or Pharisee-ism would never have been a problem. If a law had been given that could impart life, than there would have been no need for a Christ and righteousness would have been attained through legal observance (Galatians 3:21).

But the law and its instruction rather provide a "curse" of sorts (Galatians 3:13) on us because it set up standards that no one can naturally fully abide by. The Law's purpose was to provide us insight into our sin (Romans 3:20). The law was to reveal to us that we do in fact reign over others. We cannot fully love our neighbor because our natural disposition is directed toward self-reign and through the law, we are made were aware of it.

Therefore, we need a human person (because it is a human problem) who can fulfill the covenant in order for righteousness to be attained. So it is appropriate that Jesus declared that he had come not to abolish or get rid of the law or the prophets, but to fulfill them (Matthew 5:17). In other words, Jesus is the fulfillment of love for God and love for the other simply because he is the incarnation of love! Jesus encourages us to follow the ethos (love) of the law more rigorously, intentionally and holistically. He challenges us to understand what love really is.

This is evident when he professes that the greatest commandment, that which the *entirety of the law and prophets rest on*, is that we love God with our entire being (our heart, soul, mind and strength) and that we love one another as ourselves (Matthew 22:37-40). Paul echoes this understanding by stating "the entire law is fulfilled in keeping this one command: 'Love your neighbor as yourself'" (Galatians 5:14).

Love is the underlying principle of the entire Bible. Neither the law nor the prophets are separated from it. Anything that is ever said regarding a way of life in the entire Bible is directing its readers deeper into their own ability and capacity to love God and love others.

But this naturally begs the question of some of the historical writings of the Old Testament. One may appropriately ask how love infiltrates the command to go and destroy entire nations of people and to that I want to say two things.

First, God is patient. There is never an instance in all of scripture where someone failed once and consequently was destroyed. All have sinned and fallen short of God's standards (Romans 3:23) and this is not just a one-time occurrence. As has been discussed, our nature is directed against God. The "acts" of sin are not really acts at all—they are the product of a corrupt nature.

In the Old Testament we are told that God waited patiently for 400 years for the Amorites to repent before he ushered his people into the promised land at their expense (Genesis 15:13-16). We are also led to believe that those who were faithful to God were redeemed from destruction (like Rahab; also Ezekiel 14:14, 20) and that those cities that were destroyed were entirely depraved—they had firmly hardened their hearts toward God (Genesis 18:32).

In addition, once the monarchy was established in Israel, the king became the representative for the people and thus the people suffered because of the king's sins (i.e. 2 Samuel 24). Israel asking for a king was their clear rejection of God as their king. It is not as if they didn't know what they were getting themselves into:

> Listen to all that the people are saying to you; it is not you [Samuel] they have rejected, but they have rejected me [God] as their king. As they have done from the day I brought them up out of Egypt until this day, forsaking me and serving other gods, so they are doing to you. Now listen to them; but warn them solemnly and let them know what the king who will reign over them will claim as his rights [force their children into serving him; taking a tenth of everything they own]...But the people refused to listen to Samuel. "No!' they said.

'We want a king over us. Then we will be like all the other nations...' The Lord answered, 'Listen to them and give them a king'" (1 Samuel 8:6-9, 19, 21).

Israel had always been under the principle of corporate solidarity (the idea that community exists as a unit rather than a system of individuals). This is what covenant based community assumes of its participants. Therefore, the sins of an individual within that community, especially the king—the communities representative, become the sins of the whole (this is discussed in greater detail below). Or in other words, the community-unit becomes responsible for the individuals within the community.

All this is to say that while some passages seem to indicate God's wrath is instantaneous, careful reading indicates that God is patient in his judgment and does not desire to punish anyone but for all to come to repentance (2 Peter 3:9; 1 Timothy 2:4).

Second, God does not judge arbitrarily. God established a covenant between himself and all of humanity when he created the first human being. Biblical Jews understood that God created humanity as a single individual to make the point that what was and is done to a single individual is intrinsically done to the entire human race. The covenant established with Adam and Eve is implied to be a covenant with all people. As I have shown before, we share in the actions of Adam and Eve, and just as their sin becomes our sin, so do we like them, break our creation covenant with God. All of us, collectively, have chosen disobedience against God and therefore death (Genesis 2:17).

The same is true for Noah and his descendants (ultimately, us). When God makes his promise to never again flood the earth, he also renews his covenant with all of humanity including their future descendants (Genesis 9:8). But yet again, humanity chooses to break their covenant with God. Ham, Noah's youngest son, is still bent inward upon himself as can be seen by his anti-love interaction with his father. Instead of covering his father's shame and honoring him, Ham gossiped and slandered his father (Genesis 9:22) and thereby declared his superiority and power over him. Ham would eventually become the father of the Canaanites, the Assyrians, Babylonians and Egyptians (Genesis 10:6-20). These pagan nations learned from Ham how to live. They were established with a foundational relationship and covenant with God but were unable to abide in proper conduct as their lust for power became the foundation they lived off of. They too are therefore without excuse because they had been established under the creation and Noahic covenants (Romans 1:18-32).

We see the judgment of these nations portrayed in Isaiah's prophecy. They are judged because they had abandoned God in their pride, conceit, insolence, oppression, greed, gluttony, evil, murder, strife, deceit, malice and idolatry: they had abandoned covenant with God and consequently accrued punishment for their choices (Isaiah 14:28-24:23; Ezekiel 25:1-32:32). But a beautiful image is provided for when these nations repent of their many sins and turn back to God:

> In that day Israel will be the third, along with Egypt and Assyria, a blessing on the earth. The Lord Almighty will bless them, saying, 'blessed be Egypt my people, Assyria my handiwork, and Israel my inheritance' (Isaiah 19:24-25).

The nations surrounding Israel are not without hope for God is a god of inclusion. We see this in Jonah's prophecy and the repentant hearts of the Assyrians. If the Ninevites would have remained in their sin, they would have been destroyed (Nahum's prophecy) but because of their repentance, they were blessed and it was Israel, personified in Jonah, who was angry because of it, not God.

The same is true of the Israelites. Those who had received the promise of God would too be destroyed because of their unfaithfulness to God's covenant with them. The Israelites rejected God through their persistent desire and accomplishment to be like the pagan nations surrounding them (1 Samuel 8:5-7; Ezekiel 11:12). God did not choose or elect a *nation* but rather a *people type* that would receive his blessings, presence and salvation. Those who were covenantally faithful would be saved, not national Israel. Abraham received the promise because he was righteous in a land of unrighteousness and it was his descendants who would therefore receive the gift of the law. But not all who descended from Israel are Israel for it is those who are children of the promise, not of the blood line, who are Abraham's offspring (Romans 9:6-8).

God therefore did not randomly select people for the Israelites to destroy. He used various nations as rods of judgment on those who were covenantally unfaithful to him—even if these people were the nation of Israel. But it is not as if God took pleasure in this:

> Therefore, house of Israel, I will judge each of you according to your own ways, declares the Sovereign Lord. Repent! Turn away from all your offense; then sin will not be your downfall. Rid yourselves of all the offenses you have committed, and get a new heart and a new spirit. Why will you die, house of Israel? For I take no pleasure in the death of anyone, declares the Sovereign Lord. Repent and live (Ezekiel 18:30-32).

God does not judge arbitrarily.

Some might argue these are straw men's arguments but scripture is clear that humanity is judged because of the sin they willingly commit. While we focus on the "Burning anger of the Lord" images in the Old Testament, caught up in the archaic language of "The wrath of God," we miss the fact that in the Old Testament God is repeatedly characterized by the same virtues we bestow upon him in the New Testament: grace (Isaiah 26:10; Jonah 2:8), mercy (2 Samuel 24:14; 1 Chronicles 21:13; Nehemiah 9:31; Psalm 5:7), forgiveness (Exodus 23:21, 34:9; Psalm 130:4; Numbers 14:20) and love (Exodus 15:13; Numbers 14:9, 18; Deuteronomy 33:3; 1 Kings 10:9; Psalm 13:5). These are only a small sample of the many instances where God proves himself as a great God of love. The truth of the matter is we all have abandoned our covenant call to love in favor of our own self-interest and gain.

But the message underlying the entire Bible is that God's call on humanity is to reenter covenant by participating in reciprocal love with him, which then overflows to those around us. For God, to love him is to love others. The two cannot be separated.

But we separate them all the time.

Everyday there are people who proclaim to love God with their tongues but then turn around and deny that same love with their actions. If we claim to love God yet hate our neighbor, we are liars and our love for

God does not actually exist (I John 4:20). But in an attempt to justify ourselves, we beg the question "Who is my neighbor?" And instead of retelling the parable of the Good Samaritan (Luke 10:25-37), I will simply tell you its conclusion: you are to treat all people who are in need of mercy as your neighbor. Who is in need of mercy? All who have sinned, which is all of us (Romans 3:23). In other words, all people are your neighbor.

This might seem radical and indeed it is. When we fail to love the person next to us, we likewise fail to love God. But some will naturally say, "God, if I saw you in need—hungry, sick, thirsty in prison, or needing clothing—I would have given radically in order to meet *your* needs, but you are in heaven, infinite, eternal and omnipotent. My assumption that you would even be in need is a denial of who you are! Surely I cannot be judged for that!"

And he will say plainly to them, "My breath resides within the lungs of every human person, what you failed to do for them, you failed to do for me" (Matthew 25:45).

If we love God and desire to be bound to the God who is love, we must love our neighbor.

chapter seven. love and anti love (repentance)

If we love God and desire to be bound to the God who is love, we must love our neighbor.

"Hey, is anyone sitting here?" Andy already knew the answer but wanted to make a good first impression.

"No." Leila's answer was short and sweet. She only looked up at Andy for a moment before she went back to finish the text message she was working on before the bell rang.

Andy waited a moment until she was finished. "I'm Andy." He held out his hand hoping for hers in return.

"Hi. I'm Leila." She didn't have much else to say but Andy's conversational skills didn't prove to be worth much. "So, are you excited for this class?" she asked.

"Yeah, really excited! I love science classes. I hope to be a doctor so I really like biology, but physics is still fun."

"Fun? Is that how you really describe it? Is it the sort of thing you do in your free time? Like, a hobby?"

"Yeah!" Andy realized he was overly excited and calmed down. "I mean, science is one of those things you have to make fun. Like, for instance, this past summer at science camp..." Andy couldn't believe those words just came out of his mouth. His face turned immediately red, his shoulders sank and his face dropped. "I didn't mean to tell you that. I am really not that into this stuff it's just that..."

Leila interrupted. "You know what? Don't worry about it. At least you get to do things you are interested in. All I do is clean up after my dad. Now we have both said things we didn't mean to. Sorry." The ten second pause in the conversation felt like an eternity. "So, how did this camp of yours make science fun?"

Andy gave a half-smile and continued. "Well, our final assignment was to study a law of motion called inertia. Inertia basically means that if an object is in motion, it will stay in motion until a greater force acts upon it."

Leila gave a big nod and rolled her eyes. Andy was too excited about his story to notice her reactions.

"So my bunk mates and I decided we would make a film about a dummy who kept experiencing the effects of this law on his body. It was funny because whenever the dummy had to speak of his experiences, I, wearing the same clothes as the dummy spoke for him. It was hilarious!"

Leila didn't seem impressed. She simply nodded her head and gave a chuckle. Andy noticed her response. He cleared his throat and continued.

"Well, what we noticed was that inertia isn't very fun or exciting when experienced in the real world. So, we had to create experiences that would be fun and entertaining. We did things like throwing the dummy off of a roof and filming it fall apart on the ground. We would drive a car at various speeds and see if the dummy could stop the car by its mere mass. We would throw the dummy at various objects to determine in which circumstances the dummy would over-power the mass or in which circumstances it was the other way around. Like, one time, we threw the dummy at a door and noticed that the door did not budge. So instead we threw it at a tree. It was so funny because when the dummy hit the tree, his head fell off! So when I had to speak about hitting the tree, I stuffed my head into my shirt so it looked like a headless man was talking!"

Leila had to admit that Andy's quirky likes and innocence were kind of cute. He was so bashful and awkward that she, for the first time in a long time, forgot about the mess that was her life. Having such an odd, yet completely normal, conversation almost made her feel happy.

"But that wasn't even the best part! For the finale, we threw the dummy through a pane of glass from an old window we found, and the glass just went everywhere! It was fun to watch. We took some ketchup and smeared it all over my face to make it look like I had just gone head first through a window and that my face had gotten all cut up. It was pretty funny."

Leila was impressed. "It sounds like you had a lot of fun."

"Yeah, well, what was also funny is that we didn't place or even receive a medal. What we realized in the end was that although we made a funny video, we didn't really say a whole lot about inertia."

"So, your science was fun, but not very scientific?"

"Yeah, well, you know, inertia is one of those things that is difficult to understand as it is. I mean, it was a hard assignment. Like, how do you show forces changing each other and affecting one another? I mean, it was hard because..."

"...Good point." Andy gave a nervous chuckle and began to tap his pen on his desk, a habit he had when he felt stupid. He had tried so hard to make a good first impression.

"You know what, don't worry about it. It sounds way better than anything I could have d..." The bell rang as Leila was finishing her sentence.

Both of them were relieved.

At birth, we are all hurled into a particular trajectory casting away from the presence of God. This route will lead each of us deeper and deeper into ourselves seeking our own benefit, desires and needs prior to anyone else's if it is not dealt with. Our struggle comes in realizing that we cannot move our trajectory on our own. Sure, many of us try and sometimes receive the impression that we are succeeding but the truth is we will stay on our current trajectory until a force greater than ourselves knocks us off of it and redirects us in a different direction.

As we have said before, the only thing that *can* move us is something outside of ourselves—the *agape* of God, personified in Jesus Christ. Naturally, one may then ask "Were those prior to Jesus Christ without hope?" By no means. While God's *hesed* or covenantal love was fulfilled in Jesus Christ, it does not mean it was absent prior to his coming. God's call to love upon humanity was the call to repent of all that was anti-love in their lives. Today, repentance is still the call to reenter active reciprocal love with all of humanity.

The only way this can happen is through repentance—accepting the forgiveness of God, and in turn forgiving others. Remember that what took place in the Garden of Eden was not a divide or severing but merely a turning around. "To repent" literally means "to turn around." Military leaders in first century Roman armies would yell "Metanoia!" (repent!) at their soldiers if they wanted them to make an about-face. Understanding this concept of repentance is the second step to reclaiming our proper relationship to the Trinitarian God (the first being realizing our sin-nature).

But repentance is not often talked about today in our churches, or if it is, it is often characterized as passive forgiveness from sins confessed. We tell people to feel sorry for what they have done and equate this with repentance. But this is an exceptionally poor definition of what repentance actually asks of those who do it.

In our previously established theological context, "turning around" means dying to my own self-interest and reign, literally shifting my nature. In other words, repentance is not merely confession of sins or saying "I'm sorry." Repentance is not passive. The problem is that we have most prominently defined the Christian existence as only "coming back" to neutral ground (if such a place actually exists). We say, "I don't support hatred, evil and sin. That's enough, right? True, I don't necessarily fight against injustice or sacrifice myself for people I don't even know but no one has ever told me I had to. Passive participation in Christ has always been the standard. Who would participate if it were any other way?"

And if this is the case, it is very disturbing.

John the Baptist said that we must "Produce fruit in keeping with repentance...and every tree that does not produce fruit will be cut down and thrown into the fire" (Luke 3:8-9). The crowd, upon hearing these words, at least had the conviction to ask what they then must do. So John tells them what they must do: reorient your life to active love, not blind passivity. If you have two shirts, share with someone who has none and if you have food, do the same. Don't cheat one another for your own gain but be content with what you have and rather than hoarding it, give it away freely (Luke 3:11-14). I fear that many today would rather try to justify their inaction, play ignorant, or fall back on God's grace and use it as a license to continue on in their current trajectory of passivity.

But passive repentance is not repentance at all.

Neutral ground is territory occupied by the enemy.

We live in a world where two, and only two, kingdoms are present. We either occupy God's kingdom or we reign over our own. The problem is that we have come to believe we can have it both ways—that we can occupy both kingdoms, but this naturally implies a compartmentalized Christianity. We give God a portion of our lives and "repent" of various and certain actions/thoughts, but we don't repent of our nature. We give God our Sunday morning from 10:30-12:00 but then we go out into the church parking lot and rage against the congestion and "idiot drivers" who are hindering our ability to get home so we can watch yet another meaningless football game. We do our devotions ritualistically but walk away from the Word forgetting what it said on our way to the shower. We pray in hopes that God will bless us, but who really cares about the rest of the world—they can pray for themselves. We give a little of our money but give it while grumbling as we make lists of where that money could have gone to support our own needs and wants.

Easy and compartmentalized Christianity gets people in the church doors. But come on, who wants to hear that if you want any part of Christ that you must take up your cross and follow him; or if you want life that you must first die to yourself? That is scary and intimidating language. Let's not put such a heavy yoke on the people. After all, "My yoke is easy, and my burden is light" (Matthew 11:30), right? Christianity is easy! Let's ease people into discipleship through fun, relevant and appealing messages. We'll eventually come around to those harder topics once we are more "Spiritually mature."

It's almost as if we actually believe that compartmentalized topics will promote something different than a compartmentalized faith.

The problem with starting people's journey of discipleship with cheap grace is that it is indoctrinating them into a certain way of thinking: we are being formed into people who actually believe cheap grace is actual grace.

But it is not.

We are merely accepting Jesus as our savior but not as our Lord. In feudal times, the Lord ruled the everyday affairs of his people. Thus we acknowledge Jesus as our savior only and then tend to our lives sending him tribute every once and awhile instead of unswerving fealty. But Jesus condemns this: "Many will say to me on that day, 'Lord, Lord, did we not prophesy in your name and in your name drive out demons and in your name perform many miracles?' Then I will tell them plainly, 'I never knew you. Away from me, you evil doers'" (Matthew 7:22-23)! Jesus understood that many were content with providing him lip service. He is confidently declaring that for them, his eternal presence will not be a reality.

Swearing fealty meant pledging not just your material possessions but your very life—all of it. Could it be that in order to attain God that we must lay down our arms and willingly submit to him? Could it be that we must actually turn from the world and the promotion of ourselves and reorient our natures in order to gain salvation?

Because the reality is it's all or nothing.

God wants the entirety of who we are. The person who hands the entirety of their life over to God save one relationship remains in the "nothing" category. Giving 99% comes up just as short as those giving 10%, or 0%, because in saving 1% for ourselves, we are essentially proclaiming our throne is still established. We have not surrendered; we have merely sent tribute to appease the king. We have pinned our shirt to the cross and claimed to have been crucified. We have cut off an arm and claim to have died. We wear Jesus bracelets and claim to be changed. All are façades established by Satan in hopes that we would feel enough at ease with our meager offerings to not actually be Christ's tangible hands and feet to a hurting world.

The goal of the Christ-life is not simply to *do* good works but to *be* love for all people. Our goal is to reorient our lives to reciprocal love relationship: to reenter the Trinitarian God bounded in love.

In light of this, I want to propose a new definition of what sin is. Because God, who is love, is our standard and sin is that which hinders our goal, sin is everything that is in opposition to God and should therefore be defined as all that is *anti-love*. John says that "sin is lawlessness" (1 John 3:4). Consider this next to Romans 13:8-10:

Let no debt remain outstanding, except the continuing debt to love one another, for whoever loves others has fulfilled the law. The commandments, "You shall not commit adultery," "You shall not murder," "You shall not steal," "You shall not covet," and whatever other command there may be, are summed up in this one command: "Love your neighbor as yourself." Love does no harm to its neighbor. Therefore love is the fulfillment of the law.

Sin is the antithesis of love and love the antithesis of sin. Where love is absent, sin is reigning. Where we are passive in love, we are active in sin. And John goes one step further when he describes sin as not only anti-love but as active hatred. In other words, we are never passive—never. We are either active in love or active in hate.

Every act, thought or word that is non-love is active hatred.

Hatred is an intense negative emotional dissonance against another person. We typically only use language of hatred towards those people whom we really dislike. But John, in his brilliance, says that when we fail to love or when we are passive in our love for others, it is the outworking of hatred against that person (1 John 2:9-11). When my wants and desires are insisted upon above those of another person's, I am proving that my love for God is flippant and hollow. The love of God is not in me. I am loving with word and tongue but with neither truth nor action (1 John 3:18), and if my love remains in the cognitive, it is not love at all but a mere reflection of the passivity by which our culture thrives.

Consider the insights of Søren Kierkegaard from his book *Either/Or:*

> The love of God is hatred of the world, and love of the world is hatred of God. This is the colossal point of contention; either love or hate. This is the place where the most terrible fight must be fought. And where is this place? In a person's innermost being. Whether the struggle is over millions or over a penny, it is a matter of loving and preferring God.... There is a tremendous danger in which we find ourselves by being human, a danger that consists in the fact that we are placed between two tremendous powers. The choice is left to us. We must either love or hate, and not to love is to hate. So

hostile are these two powers that the slightest inclination towards the one side becomes absolute opposition to the other..."

And it seems we are caught in the middle. We are held up in a universe that has seen its redemption but strives after selfish ambition and vain conceit (Philippians 2:3).

The question you may have is appropriate: can someone, on this side of eternity, give of themselves *fully* to the kingdom of God and to self-sacrificial love? I mean, if love defeats sin and we have entered into the essence of love in Christ, does this mean we will never sin again? After all, John says that "No one who lives in him keeps on sinning. No one who continues to sin has either seen him or known him. [...] Those who are born of God will not continue to sin, because God's seed remains in them; they cannot go on sinning" (I John 3:6, 9).

And he is absolutely right.

But is this what it really sounds like, that those who follow Christ will never sin again? I don't necessarily think so. In the Greek language writers often made use of a literary devise known as the *itinerant present tense*. This means that sometimes when the present tense is used, it refers not to a single activity but to those actions done habitually or as a characterization of a person. John is describing those who have reoriented their disposition from self-reign to love. Those who have died to themselves will no longer live out of their old selves because the old is done away with (Romans 6:6). They have become a new creation in Christ: a new humanity (2 Corinthians 5:17). They are no longer slaves to self-reign and personal exaltation but now are liberated under God.

This does not mean that they will never have an expression or anti-love behavior again in their life. It simply means that they are defined by their love rather than their sin, and when they sin, they acknowledge it and repent of it. Remember that repentance necessitates an active denial of that sin in their life. They turn around from that particular behavior because it is the degradation of their new-found humanity and they will do this moment-in and moment-out for the rest of their natural lives.

The thing that separates those who have reoriented their lives to Christ from those who have not is not necessarily the outworking of their "being good people" simply because that is a relativistic concept (as has been discussed before) but the acknowledgment of their sin and the constant striving after repentance—the turning from anti-loving behavior towards the face of God in love for him and love other others. A drunkard who understands his plight and error, yet repents after each failure, growing and striving after love and therefore growing in the cessation of his error is far closer to God than the church-bound Pharisee who thinks he has nothing to repent of.

Re-orienting our disposition to God and love does not mean we will love in every situation or be perfect—at least on this side of eternity. It simply means we will acknowledge our failure, pick ourselves up and by God's grace, do it differently next time: we repent. The person who sins minimally and moves on with their life as if they are sinless is a much different person than the one who sins continually but knows of their plight and is seeking by God's grace and Spirit to correct themselves. The person who is actually repenting will one day find themselves victorious over sins that once held them down. Just because that day might not be tomorrow does not mean we should absolve ourselves from trying.

Love and repentance require that we continue to take steps forward.

After all, it is a journey. We are a work in progress. Our search for God in love is a much greater quest than any of us probably understand.

And it begins now.

chaptereight.lifeanddeath//loveandantilove
(meaning)

Our search for God in love is a much greater quest than any of us probably understand.

And it begins now.

Life and Love and Why

Andy awoke to his first day of summer vacation already feeling weary because of the daunting task that lay before him. He had just finished his first year of college and had vowed to spend the first three hours of everyday throughout his summer studying, anticipating the difficulty of his pre-med classes in the fall.

He had decided to move back into his childhood home in order to save money and so his attention would not be divided. His parents and his brother, John, were in Minnesota this summer, something they had done many times before, but never for the whole summer. Though Andy appreciated the peace and quiet, solitude was not something he was accustomed to, living with Mark for the past nine months. The feeling unsettled him a little. As he stumbled out of bed, he longed to be back at school.

He had gotten in late the night before, and as soon as he got home he went straight to his new bedroom and crashed from exhaustion. Upon his entrance to college, John had moved into his old room, the bigger one closer to the bathroom. Thus, Andy was cramped into his little brother's room for three months. It didn't feel much like home that morning. Yawning, he walked to the corner desk to begin what promised to be a very long summer.

But he couldn't settle down to study.

Something was odd.

It wasn't the room, its smell, the way the light came in or the house in general but something more internal to who he was. He noticed that he greatly disliked—was even uncomfortable with the way his brother had chosen to decorate his room. He had almost forgotten that his little brother once had an infatuation with clowns and the circus.

Andy looked intently at the clowns on the wall and their eager grimaces. Some clowns were juggling while others were doing cartwheels. Each clown looked similar in that they all had puffy red hair, white faces with bright red noses. They were all wearing blue body suits with yellow polka-dots with oversized red shoes. Each had a certain demonic look in *their eyes that Andy could not quite interpret but as he stared, he was sure something evil lurked in their minds.*

But the clowns didn't stop with the wallpaper.

There were clown dolls on shelves, clown lamps at his desk, a clown rug on the floor, a clown clock on the wall. Clowns swung from ropes attached to the ceiling, clown faces were on the ceiling fan blades. The bed sported a faded clown pillow case and a clown comforter. Their leering faces creeped him out, and made him question his brother's sanity. What was with this idolatry of clowns? No wonder he moved.

Andy decided that clowns were not good company for a mature man's scientific study. And so he set out to find a new corner of the house that would be more conducive to his mission. He made his way to the coffee pot, brewed a cup, and sat down at the kitchen table.

As he stared at the biology book in front of him, willing its contents to meld with his mind, he noticed how the light from the window slanted so brilliantly across the page. What a difference than his maniacal clown room. He went to the window, coffee cup in hand, in hopes that the sun would give him the energy to stop procrastinating.

But what he saw threw away all thoughts of study.

A girl hurried through his front lawn with the clear intention of fleeing something—or someone. She kept looking over her shoulders as if she thought she was being followed.

Andy immediately recognized the girl. It was Leila, the girl he had sat next to in physics class his senior year of high school. Nobody knew this—and Andy himself was hesitant to admit it—but he had been in love with Leila since the eighth grade.

The story of the Bible begins in the Garden of Eden and the creation of all that exists. For the purpose of this book, I will not attempt to understand how this process took place. What is far more interesting is the interaction between God and the first human person.

The story tells us that once the garden was completed, God made a man from the dirt, gave him life and put him in the garden to till the soil, plant the seed, care for the crops and tend to the harvest. Adam was free to eat of any tree in the garden except the tree of the knowledge of good and evil. God told Adam specifically that if he ate from this tree, *he would die* (Genesis 2:17).

What I find most interesting about this warning is that Adam understood what God was talking about. As far as scripture tells us, death did not seem to exist in any form at the time God gave him this command. Adam, however, knew enough about death to communicate the injunction to Eve, for, when she was asked by the serpent if God actually said they would die, she answered in the affirmative. Somehow, Adam and Eve knew what death was without ever experiencing it. Thus, it seems that they had a particular understanding of what death was.

The serpent tells them that they will not die and through their continued discussion, they believe that the serpent is telling the truth. Somehow, what they would experience from their eating of the tree would not be death as they understood it but something else. God's definition of death and theirs did not correspond.

God is not a liar, so when God says, "You will surely die," I can only assume that when Adam and Eve ate of the tree, an actual death occurred. In turning around in disobedience and self-exaltation, the essence of God in love—the source of life itself—was lost and no longer sustained them.

They had died.

What flows from this one act of disobedience and death has governed every decision made by every human person since that point.

Every decision made is a decision in hope to reclaim life.

Everyone is searching for God. Most people just don't know it.

You may think this preposterous for you could probably make a list as long as your arm of people who made foolish choices that did not lead to life. I could do the same, but the choice for life as perceived by the maker of the decision does not necessitate that life flows from that act; it simply necessitates that in making a particular decision, they thought life would be found.

But life has been lost. We are now in eager pursuit of finding it. The difficulty is that our minds have been twisted by the lie that life is found in our attempt to "be like God," our self-reign. Sin whispers in our ear that it can make us happy. "Watch out for yourself," it says. "As long as you are content, warm, well-fed, clothed and happy, you have found life. Do whatever makes you feel good about yourself. Don't worry about the consequences. When consequences arise, skirt around them or interact with them in a way that makes you feel good, happy and content. Do whatever it takes to achieve for yourself what you desire. Does drinking make you feel good or minimize your emotional pain? Well, you have found a source of life. Does pornography or sex appeal to your emotions, make you feel wanted and loved? Well, do it. Isn't your happiness the point of it all? Does having the nicest and trendiest clothes, car and house make you feel important and happy? Strive, strive, strive then to meet your goals, gain your paycheck and spend your money. Oh, you have to work seventy-five hours a week to provide your family with the kind of lifestyle they want? Well, life is found in having fun and with having the most toys. Work is the cost of happiness."

Every choice we make is a choice for perceived life. We will choose pizza over a salad for lunch every day because pizza tastes good even if it is slowly killing us. And when we are frustrated or in need of comfort, the pizza is always there. Or we choose Salad because we know that pizza will not help us attain a body like those of the models in magazines. And because we know that perfect bodies are what is desired, we will go to great lengths to attain them, even if it means starving ourselves. After all, looking a certain way makes us feel good and wanted by the opposite sex—and in our culture, isn't that what life is really about?

We will drive the nicest cars because we know that luxury is a status symbol and we love to be seen for what we have. We will decorate our houses like those in magazines because we love it when people admire what we have. Many do this even though they know they cannot afford to. Many do this even though they know that their money should be spent elsewhere. The life of luxury, for some, is greater than the fear of debt.

I cannot be exhaustive in my examples but the reality is every decision—no matter how small it is—is a decision for life, or meaning, or purpose, or happiness. We are people who run away from death at all costs. But this doesn't mean we are any more alive because of it. Some people have suffered so much that they are willing to run from all that they have ever known because it had only brought them pain. Some, sadly, make decisions toward life through cutting, embedding and for some, even death itself becomes their search for life.

One time too many.

Leila angrily ripped off her covers and grabbed some sweats. Downstairs, she could hear the dull thuds and sharp claps of blows, and slurred yelling. Her father was home again. Something ceramic crashed. She knew he hadn't come home the night before, which meant he had spent the entire night bar-hopping and paying for lap-dances.

This morning, Leila had had enough. She knew that when he was finished with her mother, she would be next.

Her father beat her and could have cared less that she was alive. Her mother, the walking emotional zombie, had completely neglected her for as long as she could remember. With these thoughts in mind, she grabbed her knock-off Jansport, threw in a change of clothes and her wallet, and crawled out her bedroom window. She was headed to the bus station, which took her through the yard of Andy Moore, the boy she used to sit next to in physics class.

Our human nature compels us toward self-preservation not because of some evolutionary biological function but because we have been taught that in self-gratification is the source of life.

Our society confirms this. We are constantly being told that we can and should find meaning, happiness, joy, fulfillment and life in our culture, our world and our own happiness. Simply listen to the implied and overt messages told through commercials and store slogans over the years:

Herbergers: this department store asks that we "Give More, Give Joy."[xi] The implied message is that joy is found in giving material possessions purchased from Herbergers to our loved ones. Our joy is intrinsically connected to the stuff we have and the stuff we are able to give.

JC Penny: this department store tells us "It's All Inside."[xii] Evidently, all we will ever need in life can be purchased at this store. "All" must mean happiness, fulfillment and possibly pleasure alongside clothing and random gadgets.

Sears: this department store assures us they have "The Good Life at a Great Price. Guaranteed."[xiii] The good life must come with the products they sell—evidently cheaper than their competitors. And it is not *a* good life but *the* good life as if all life outside of Sears pales in comparison to what they can offer.

Kmart: this big-box store says it has "The Stuff of Life."[xiv] Kmart products evidently hold the essence of life, i.e. material possessions.

Best Buy: this electronics store simply says, "You. Happier."[xv] My happiness is tied up in the DVDs I own, the TVs I watch them on, the gaming system I play and the accessories that go along with all of them.

Arby's: this fast food restaurant claims that "Happiness Is Just a Curly Fry Away."[xvi] While food can make us satisfied, all happiness is conditioned upon the state of our stomach.

Walmart: this big-box store tells us to "Save money. Live better."[xvii] The quality of life is intrinsically connected to the amount of money we have. By spending money at this store on things we probably don't actually need, we save money.

As you can see, we are constantly being told that our purpose and happiness are bound up in the things we have and the way they make us feel. If my life was fulfilled and the breadth of happiness realized in a curly fry, wouldn't I seek to eat every meal at Arby's for the rest of my life? If the fullness and best possible life attainable could be found at Sears, wouldn't everything I own be purchased from there? Wouldn't I be knocking down their doors in order to simply breathe the air that Sears has to offer? If materialism were the actual source of life, wouldn't we have discovered meaning and happiness already? Wouldn't life be great already?

Why is it that the Christmas present I wanted so badly as a child—the one I begged for and cried over—only entertained me for three days before it went into the toy chest? The box it came in entertained me longer than the actual toy did.

There is a lovely little book in the middle of the Old Testament describing how a wise man had sought meaning and fulfillment in the things of the world. He built himself a palace, planted vineyards, gardens and parks. He acquired vast amounts of cattle, gold and silver. He had for himself whatever women his eyes desired and became the most important person in all the land. It says he refused his heart no pleasure. But when he stepped back to examine all he had made, all that his work had accomplished and all the women he had taken as his own, he noticed that everything was meaningless. It was if he had been chasing after the wind (Ecclesiastes 2:1-11).

He had gained nothing.

These things could not bring him meaning for they were temporal; he could not take them with him when he died. He had toiled his whole life and invested himself in all these tasks for the sheer pleasure and respect that came with them. But he noticed that his end would be the same as everyone else's: the grave is always victorious.

His most interesting realization was born from his understanding of why we toil after achievements and pleasures: they all "spring from one person's envy of another. This too is meaningless, a chasing after the wind" (Ecclesiastes 4:4). He profoundly equates our search for life with our search for superiority and self-reign. One only "keeps up with the Jones'" because they want to be seen as respected and important as compared to their neighbors, friends and mere acquaintances. But with every act of self-exaltation is the equal but opposite act of other-degradation. It is simply another face of sin.

Sometime in the distant past, life had been lost. All people, at all times have been eagerly looking for it ever since. The problem is that we are trying to fill the void that was left with objects that by nature do not fit its shape. Because the essence of God in love—the source of life itself—was lost, our void is in the shape of our creator. Blaise Pascal said, "There is a God-shaped vacuum in the heart of every man which cannot be filled by any created thing, but only by God, the Creator, made known through Jesus." We are stuffing our vacuum with objects that by nature do not fit its shape. They give us the perception of fulfillment/meaning but in actuality they will always leave us unfulfilled.

For simplicity's sake, let us say that the God-shaped void is square and that the shape of those things we attempt to find life in (sex, popularity, money, body image, clothes, cars, etc.) are circles:

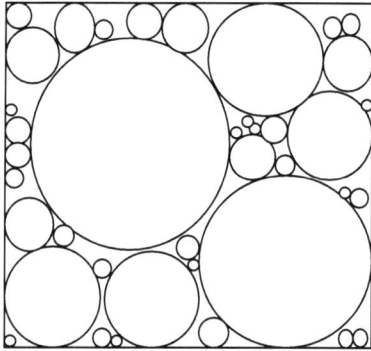

No model is perfect but ask yourself this question: if the circles represent what we fill our lives with, and if we had an infinite number of sizes to represent how much time and energy we invest in the different areas of our lives, and we also had an infinite number of circles to squash into our square, how many circles would it take to perfectly fill the square?

The reality is that it would take an infinite amount of circles. In other words, circles, by their nature, never perfectly fill a square. They might come very close, so much in fact that it appears the square is full, but by their very nature, circles will never fit 90-degree angles. In the same way, material things of this world will never satisfy the desire for fulfillment or the longing for meaning.

They were never intended to.

Creation was never meant to sustain itself.

chapter nine. the source of life in love
(purpose)

Creation was never meant to sustain itself.

"Leila! Leila!" Andy shouted as he ran down the block at a dead sprint now in need of catching his breath. Leila turned around to see who was following her and when she realized it wasn't her dad, she stopped and waited for Andy to catch up to her. "Hey, its Andy...we used to sit next to one another in physics class. You walked across my lawn a block back and you looked like you were in trouble." Andy figured he needed a better excuse to chase after her than that he was secretly in love with her.

"Yea, I remember you." She said hesitantly as she continually looked over Andy's shoulder making sure that her dad was not coming up behind them. "No, I am not in trouble; I am just in a rush. I am late to catch a bus that is leaving. I am going to live with my Grandmother for the summer." But the look on her face and her anxious looking behind him convinced Andy she was not telling him the truth.

As Andy spoke he turned around to see what Leila was looking for. "Are you sure you are alright? Who are you running from?"

"Yea, I am fine. Thanks for your concern though." But she couldn't wipe the anxiety and fear off her face or out of her eyes.

"Leila, come on." Andy said with a little authority in his voice. "What's wrong?"

Leila put her head in her hands and began to cry. "Okay! I woke up this morning to my dad hitting my mom and I feared that if I stayed, I would be next so I am running away! I hate him!" Leila screamed so loud that there was little doubt she woke up the neighbors.

Andy thought for a minute as he put his arm around Leila to console her. "My parents are gone for the next two months. Come stay at my place, at least for a little while until you know where you are going. No one will know; you can literally stay inside for the next month if you want to."

It was an appealing offer. Leila knew she had only a little money and no idea of where she was going, how she would eat, where she would sleep, or what she would do when she got to where ever it was she would end up. And so she took the offer.

Andy proved to be a gentlemen and a generous host. Leila had never known what it was like to be wanted or desired by someone. She thought it was nice. But living in such close proximity with a boy who had been in love with her and showed it by his continual chivalry proved more tempting than either of them was able to bear. It didn't take but a few weeks before they were sleeping together.

By the end of the month, just two days before Andy's parents were scheduled to come home, Leila broke the news to Andy. "I am pregnant." The silence that ensued seemed to amplify her pounding heart. "And I will not abuse this child through abortion; I will not be like my parents! I want to keep the baby."

Andy was committed to Leila, he had been for the past five years but he was afraid of what his parents would say. After all, he invited an old acquaintance to live in their house while they were gone whom he slept with and got pregnant, all the while lying to them every week over the phone about his studies, his life and what was going on in their house. He was left with two options. The first would be to wait until his parents got home and explain everything to them or he could flee now and avoid the shame that came along with everything he did.

He rightly chose the first.

His parents were disappointed—that may be an understatement—but eventually supportive. But they were determined that this child would not be born out of wedlock even though it had already been conceived in such. And so Andy and Leila were married in a simple yet legal ceremony at city hall.

They were fortunate enough to get into a married apartment on campus at Andy's college so that he could finish his degree in hopes to make a decent life for him and his family. They were doing well as a young married couple—still living off the euphoria of the past ten months—when the baby came.

They had a girl. They named her Hannah for they had been met with grace.

Andy's schedule, however, proved to be demanding. He spent each day in class and each night in study and with little sleep, he found that he and Leila were becoming increasingly irritable towards one another.

Leila, never having such a grave responsibility, was unsure of how to raise a child and be a wife and found herself becoming anxious with life, her husband and her daughter. She had no idea how to be a parent. Neither her mother nor her father modeled love or sacrifice to her, and she was therefore completely unaware of what her own daughter required from her. This led her to resent the loss of her freedom as a young woman. She began to wonder what she had missed out on: the party's, the clubs, the friends and other men. She was not ready or desiring of the responsibility of motherhood to be placed on her shoulders. Her ancient longing to not be like her parents seemed too distant a memory to creep back into her mind. And so Leila did the one thing she knew how to do.

She ran.

Andy awoke one March morning to a crying baby and a letter from Leila simply saying, "I am sorry. I cannot stay." Andy tried to raise Hannah on his own but found the task of balancing school with a new job and caring for her to be too difficult. He decided he would put his school work on hold for a couple of years while he tried to make enough money to support his daughter. What he quickly noticed was that the jobs he was qualified to do did not pay well and this forced him to take on a second shift. His parents were gracious enough to watch Hannah during his night shift which essentially paid him enough money to pay for her daycare during his first.

Three years of sleepless nights, long hours, small paychecks and never seeing his daughter took its toll on Andy. It wasn't long before the happiness he once found in life vanished. Because the reality of life was too big a burden for him to endure, he began to evade it through drinking. He spent most of his day—even while at work—either hung over from the night before or getting drunk. Every extra dollar he could find went to another bottle because somehow when he was drinking, he felt like a new man, a better man; someone who was alive.

And he hated himself when he was sober.

The main story of the Old Testament book of Exodus centers on the Israelites liberation from Egyptian slavery. Because of the miraculous acts of God performed by Moses, they were able to escape slavery and follow a God-given path to the Promised Land.

But the people were not content.

On the forty-fifth day of travel they grumbled and complained that their conditions were not worth their freedom. They said it would have been better if they would have stayed enslaved under the Egyptians because at least there they sat around pots of meat and vegetables (Exodus 16:3). God, upon hearing the complaints of his people said he would rain down bread from heaven for them. Each day they could go out and gather off the ground one day's worth of bread for themselves and their families.

Some enterprising members of the community, however, wanted to gather enough for a couple of days at a time so they wouldn't have to go out and pick every day.

But an interesting thing happened. When they awoke the second day to retrieve the day-old bread they had gathered, they saw that it was full of maggots and mold.

The bread they had put their hope in did not last them but one day. It could not sustain them.

In John 6:25-28, Jesus comments on this story. Peasants from all around the region had begun to follow Jesus because he had recently made bread fall from the sky (John 6:1-15). If you were a starving peasant and one day listened to a man who could make bread fall from the sky, I'm willing to bet you would also be following Jesus around.

But Jesus calls them on it.

They weren't following Jesus because of who he was; they were following him hoping to be fed again. "But don't you remember," Jesus says, "the bread I gave you only sustained you for a day, if I gave you more, you would eventually be hungry again. But I can give you bread that will sustain you forever, you will never again be hungry; you will never again thirst."

And at this the people got really excited. "Please! Always give us this bread."

And so Jesus tells them, "I am the bread of life...I am the bread that came down from heaven. Your ancestors ate manna in the wilderness and yet they died. But if you eat of my flesh and drink of my blood, you will live forever."

During the first couple centuries after Jesus' earthly ministry, there were three major negative claims regarding his followers. The first was that they were incestuous because they called their own spouses "brother and sister." The second was that they were atheistic because they worshiped an invisible God. The third was that they were cannibalistic because they took part in communion "love feasts" where they "ate of Christ's flesh and drank of his blood."

As for the first accusation, believers were of course referring to their being brothers and sisters in Christ, not literally of the same mother and father. As for the second, during this time in history, if you didn't have an image of your god, you didn't have a god. Thus, by worshiping a God with no iconic referent, the Christians were deemed atheistic.

But as for the third, the language of eating and drinking of Christ's body and blood would have brought the mind of the Jew to the sacrificial system: "...the gifts and sacrifices being offered...are only a matter of food and drink and various ceremonial washings—external regulations..." (Hebrews 9:9-10). The old system of sacrifice was merely a shadow of the perfect sacrifice that was to come, namely Jesus Christ. Taking of Jesus body and blood therefore *signified* participation with his perfect sacrifice. Jews believed that the life force of a person or an animal was in their blood (Leviticus 17:11) and therefore it must not be eaten of. Here in this passage in John, however, Jesus is not telling his people to literally drink his blood but to take upon themselves his life.

Enter into my sacrifice.

Transform into my image, my life.

There is no life outside of Jesus Christ. When the Israelites stock-piled manna so they wouldn't have to gather it every day, they found that it was moldy and full of maggots. This was not because the bread God provided wasn't well preserved but because the manna was a tangible symbol of their daily dependence on God. They were never supposed to find enduring sustenance in anything but God himself.

In the same way, the message of "Eat of me" is not a grotesque cannibalistic ritual, but a declaration to find our being, purpose, fulfillment and sustenance in the person of Jesus Christ.

Unfortunately, the response Jesus received from the five-thousand was shocking. All who had watched the bread fall from the sky and therefore followed Jesus left him in this moment. They only followed because of what they could get out of it. They might have been a follower of him, but Jesus was willing to test their commitment and says "Put aside everything else, do not seek sustenance in the ways of this world, and do not look for meaning and purpose in temporal things. Tomorrow when you look to them, they will be moldy, maggot filled, broken, rusty, dead and destroyed.

They do not last.

Look only to me."

The teaching was too hard for those who sought only to be fed. And in one last plea Jesus asks the faithful twelve, "Are you going to leave too?"

Their response was beautiful.

"Lord, to whom shall we go? You have the words of eternal life" (John 6:68).

It didn't take long before Andy was unable to perform the necessary duties his job called for. Although he was able to hide his being hungover through solitude and mouth wash while at work, his job performance was becoming clumsy.

And his boss took notice.

It was eventually uncovered that Andy had been coming to work hungover if not intoxicated and he was quickly fired. The frustration of losing his job and any hope of supporting his daughter sent him looking for an escape and low and behold, his liquor cabinet would not fail him. But something odd happened as he opened his cabinet. For the first time, he saw the alcohol for what it was: not an escape from the pain of the world but much of the cause for the pain he had felt.

He had hit bottom and with that a newfound perspective on life. Andy worked hard for the next couple of months getting his life back together but with his history of working intoxicated, it was very difficult for him to find employment and on top of that, he was becoming ill.

Andy knew he needed help and thought the old church on the corner would be a good start.

And so one spring day, Andy took his daughter by her hand and went to the stone laid corner church. They walked up the freshly swept, cobblestones staircase under the beautiful stained glass depicted saints and made their way to the front door—the entrance to what seemed to be the Garden of Eden: a beautiful representation of the fullness and love of God. Andy pounded on the door and when it was opened, he pleaded his case for compassion, sympathy and love to a man in a black robe.

But he received nothing of the sort.

Instead he was reprimanded for his search for mercy and told he was a liar, a manipulator, a drunk and that his kind did not belong there.

His emotions flared up and all the progress he had made over the last three months meant nothing as he was now convinced that happiness was not attainable and it didn't matter how hard he worked, nobody could help him nor did anybody want to, not even God.

And so he left, brought Hannah to his mother's house and went to the liquor store, frustrated, hurt and calloused toward feeling. He didn't wait until he got home to drink but began and finished while driving.

It was two hours later when Andy's mother received a phone call from the local police indicating that Andy had run a red light and collided at an estimated fifty miles an hour with a semi-truck that was making a left turn.

He had died on impact.

Hannah lived with her grandmother until she was seven years old and her grandmother died. For the next five years she was tossed between seven foster families and orphanages because "she was an intolerable, misbehaved girl who wouldn't listen to authority," or so was the common cry of the families when she was returned to the orphanage.

She was a girl who had never been loved and never shown attention. She knew she was a burden to all the grownups she had ever known. Her mom abandoned her when she was an infant. Her father never saw her or paid attention to her. Her Grandmother always complained that she never should have come into the world in the first place and that she only burdened everyone she came in contact with. The foster families didn't love her, show her patience or care for her up-bringing. Hannah knew she wasn't worth anything: it was all she had ever been taught about herself.

But an interesting thing started to happen when she was twelve years old: her body began to develop in ways that were completely foreign to her and that were still completely foreign to the vast majority of girls at her school. Because this was the case, Hannah noticed that older boys at her school started paying attention to her—the only attention she had ever received in life—and she liked it. She also noticed that the freer she was with her body, the more attention she received from the older boys at her school. And so she became incredibly giving.

Life and Love and Why

It wasn't long before she began kissing these boys but her being starved for attention would not allow her to stop at kissing—she finally felt loved, needed, desired and breaking through all her life's memories there was, for what seemed to be the first time in her life, a glimmer of happiness.

Three years later and countless boyfriends, at the young age of fifteen, Hannah gave birth to a baby girl. She named her Hope, for Hannah's desire was that her daughter's life would be better than her own.

Life has been lost. But we should not interpret this as being without hope. For God, the source of life, has left his mark upon us. Some might call this mark the conscience, others the universal law of right behavior and still others, the soul. John Calvin, a reformation theologian called it the *sensus divinitatis,* a natural, innate sense of the divine. But it is much more than just an idle, or passive, sense. Somehow, this conscience seeks its source—it is being prompted by someone or something to come home.

The difficulty lies in that the promptings are deafened by the nature of the environment in which they live—the fallen world. The world and its prince are seducing the human conscience by appealing to its nature of self-reign (2 Corinthians 4:4). By its very nature, the inclination to return to its source is at odds with what humanity has become and what humanity is now naturally inclined to search after (itself). What is most disturbing about this is that all too often the human nature now searches after the fabrication of life in charades and shadows rather than the true source—agape love.

I suppose this is because the real search asks for more than what most people are willing to give. Love requires—it does not suggest—that we die to the search for life outside of God, in other words, die to ourselves.

Meaning, joy, fulfillment and life can only be found in the God who is love. The source of life is the source of love in our world and therefore only in our love—the giving of ourselves for the betterment of another— will the sinful nature and the death that accompanies it be defeated and life found: "Anyone who does not love remains in death" (I John 3:14).

Life and Love and Why

The choice is ours. Life and death are both options on the table. "I have set before you life and death, blessings and curses. Now choose life, so that you and your children may live and that you may love the Lord your God, listen to his voice, and hold fast to him. For the Lord is your life..." (Deuteronomy 30:19-20).

If you remember the story of the wise man from Ecclesiastes, he was searching for life, purpose and meaning in anything and everything he could get his hands on.

But he never found it.

At the very end of the book, something profound is said of its resting place: "Now all has been heard; here is the conclusion of the matter: Fear God and keep his commandments, for this is the fulfillment of every human being" (Ecclesiastes 12:13).

Right now and with every approaching moment, Jesus is asking you a question, "Are you too going to abandon me? Will you continue to search for life where it cannot be found?"

I hope your response will be beautiful.

"Lord, where else would we go? You and you alone have the words of eternal life."

chapter ten. the purpose of pain (evil)

"Lord, where else would we go? You and you alone have the words of eternal life."

Life and Love and Why

Dan could barely open his eyes as he looked across his bedroom to the giant red numbers. 3:04 a.m. seared into his retinas. He wasn't sure how long Leila had been crying. All he knew was that he was no longer sleeping and therefore no longer happy.

Frustrated and steaming, Dan threw his comforter off, swung his legs around and slammed them to the floor. Angered, Dan stomped across the room to where Leila's basinet was.

He took a deep breath.

Staring into Leila's eyes three weeks after she was born did not give Dan the same euphoric sense it did the day he first met her. In fact, Dan hadn't slept in a week and the progress he had made to resist his old life wasn't proving to be worth much. Meg appreciated who he was starting to become but there was a real part of Dan that both liked who he used to be and didn't think it was wrong.

This was in part because he was now back at work surrounded by his old friends, environments and temptations. Alcohol was a common friend to his co-workers as well to himself and on many occasions, they all went to its source to relieve themselves of the stress of a long work day.

This particular night, looking down at Leila as she cried unceasingly, Dan's heart did not lead him to compassion as it had the few nights before. It rather brought him to annoyance, frustration and abandonment of everything he had learned about himself as a father.

He thought his ride to the hospital and the experience of being a father changed him. He thought he had finally found happiness. But he was wrong. What he thought about his past, his parents, Meg, Leila and himself did not translate to the world he knew when he returned home from the hospital. Old habits die hard and Dan was quickly drawn back into them.

Dan was a hardened man. All he knew of life was abuse, pain and hurt. Not even the innocence of his own child broke him of what he always knew to be true.

"A farmer went out to sow his seed...some fell along rocky places, where it did not have much soil. It sprang up quickly, because the soil was shallow. But when the sun came up, the plants were scorched, and they withered because they had no root" (Mark 4:5-6).

The reality of the human condition is such that few people have the capacity to receive the prompting of God to change their lives. We have been taught, especially within our current culture, to fill our lives with those things that make us happy. We therefore stuff our lives with those circles that can never fit the square of our need for fulfillment.

So when the seed of God's Spirit in love falls upon our hearts that might give us the strength and capacity to change, there is little room left for it to take root and therefore its life exists only as a flash in the pan: a spark, not a consuming fire.

Only a fleeting happiness.

Now, there may be true experiences of joy and the presence of God but often those instances are surrounded by selfish ambition. Therefore, as we have discussed earlier, what we interpret as joyous "God-filled" experiences often find their source in the exaltation of the self rather than their true source in God. When numerous people experience joy, then, their first inclination is not to drop everything and seek whole-heartedly after God but rather to continue on in their merry way looking for another experience of fleeing happiness. They interpret their joy from their own achievements, their own glorification, not God's. Thus all the victories in life that seemingly raise them above another person, look similar to Joy but only in the way salt water looks like fresh water. They have similar qualities but they come from two entirely different sources (James 3:11).

In the Judaic understanding, joy is directly correlated with the presence of God. It is not mere happiness. After all, our culture tells us we don't need God to make us happy. We don't want living water from God (John 4:10, 14; Revelation 21:6; 22:17) because we are convinced we don't need it. This even though we unceasingly search for happiness and yet remain unsatisfied.

We never make the effort to taste and see if the Lord is good (Psalm 34:8).

We prefer the taste of death; of hell.
C.S. Lewis said in his brilliant work, *The Great Divorce*, that "all that are in Hell, choose it. Without that self-choice there could be no Hell. No soul that seriously and constantly desires joy will ever miss it. Those who seek find. To those who knock it is opened."[xviii]

And so instead of giving of ourselves to Joy in love and therefore experiencing the source of life in God, we rather stuff our lives as tightly as we can with circles that were never intended to fit into a square hole. We are content with mere happiness. But happiness comes in waves and is therefore fleeting—it ought not to define us because it finds its source in the self, not God. Happiness is a fabricated emotion; it is not natural but comes with worldly things and therefore when the worldly things pass away, so does our happiness. Joy, on the other hand, is grounded in the unchanging God and therefore when our circumstances change, our Joy does not. We will have "learned the secret of being content in any and every situation, whether well fed or hungry, whether living in plenty or in want" (Philippians 4:12).

Because happiness is a distant cousin of Joy and they therefore have similar qualities, however, we are often content with its life even though its life is not true. Happiness is a stronger emotion than joy but only in the way a spark is brighter than embers.

But only one can be fanned into flame.

We therefore stuff our lives with those things that weren't made to fit our God shaped vacuum and in the process become hardened and calloused to the very thought of a God who desperately loves us and merely asks for our love in return. This because with every action we take we are actively denying the truth of his being and becoming people hardened in our denial of him.

Every choice made and experience had will form us into one of two types of people: one who is either bent more towards the self or more towards love. A person who by constant repetition chooses their own self interest at the sake of others will one day find that they cannot—or will not—make a decision to the contrary. Jesus said that these type of people do not have "eyes to see or ears to hear." They have the faculties of which those capabilities require but they are unable to use them. When we have hardened ourselves through lifelong decisions for the self we are slowly deafening our ears and blinding our eyes to the voice and sight of God.

We are the outcome or formation of an infinite amount of choices made by every human person that has ever existed from the beginning of human history. Some refer to this as chaos theory or the butterfly effect: the idea that if a butterfly were to flap its wings in the United States, the simple movement of air juxtaposed with the ensuing effects would potentially cause a typhoon in Southern Asia.

If tomorrow morning you were to sleep through your alarm for three minutes, the rest of your life would be different than if you would have woken up when it went off. Have you ever stopped to think why you and the person next to you just so happened to be at the same place at the same time? What decisions were made, not only by the two of you but by all people throughout world history the contributed to this encounter?

It will make your head hurt.

We can never know what would have happened if different choices had been made. We can, however, take a hold of our choices and begin to see the severity of them not only on ourselves but also all people. I would hope this realization would make us more intentional with the way we live our lives.

And hopefully more loving.

Because everything is interconnected.

Nothing is truly autonomous. Paul understood that it was the formation from the numerous choices for the self that lead people away from the knowledge of God:

> For although they knew God, they neither glorified him as God nor gave thanks to him, but their thinking became futile and their foolish

hearts were darkened. Although they claimed to be wise, they became fools and exchanged the glory of the immortal God for images made to look like mortal man and birds and animals and reptiles. Therefore, God gave them over in the sinful desires of their hearts to sexual impurity for the degrading of their bodies with one another. They exchanged the truth of God for a lie, and worshiped and served created things rather than the creator" (Romans 1:21-25).

Their hearts have been hardened. The difficulty with a hardened heart is that it is no longer moldable. It has been solidified and formed and although there is still hope for re-formation or transformation, this hope, now, comes at a price.

As C.S. Lewis said, "God whispers to us in our pleasures, speaks in our conscience, but shouts in our pain: it is His megaphone to rouse a deaf world."[xix] It is only by the shattering of what one has put their hope in that revival can take place. Only when the circles are destroyed will there be room for growth in a different shape, a different direction.

The tearing of the false soul away from the body will never feel good and it will always be painful. But if the soul is a fabrication of what was always intended to be there in the first place, that tearing is a necessary process for real life to begin.

Pain, in other words, is often times purposeful. This does not mean, however, it *always* finds its source in God. Its source is actually rather mysterious.

The Book of Job was written in part to clarify that there is no formula for why certain things happen to certain people. In their contemporary Judaic understanding, Job was the most unlikely candidate for the pain and suffering he experienced.

He was "blameless and upright; he feared God and shunned evil" (Job 1:1). The Jews believed that suffering was the effect of sin in one's life. This was the "wisdom" of Job's friends, the ones who tried to reason with him as to why he experienced the pain he did. But they didn't know any better than Job did. None of them could see the world from God's perspective, beyond their own finite view. But God, the one who laid the

earth's foundations, told the sea's pulsing shores where to stop, commands the sun to rise from the horizon, walks among the abode of light, the storehouses of snow, hail, rain and lightning (Job 38) can see the world from an infinite perspective. He sees all people for who they really are.
He knows us. He is our creator. Intimate.

We live in a chaotic and often times messy system of sin and redemption. Because we do not exist on islands or in a vacuum, my choice for self-reign will adversely affect someone else.

Again, when I take, someone else has to give.

And when my taking is the result of my own self-priority, I am in the wrong. I have actively hated. I have actively sinned. My actions will bump up against the actions of others and when seven billion people are actively participating in this mix, the source of pain and suffering create a mystery for us who cannot see the world from above and from all angles.

It is mysterious from our perspective simply because the puzzle is too big. Our finite view often times cannot even see the pieces of the puzzle let alone its final form. We do not have the mind or eyes of God. But its mystery does not negate that something beautiful can be born from it.

Pain, trial and suffering are purposeful because every experience we have forms us into who we become—the good ones and the bad ones equally—because we know that the "Testing of [our] faith develops perseverance. Perseverance must finish its work so that [we] may be complete, not lacking in anything" (James 1:3-4). Perseverance is not mere endurance. We must not simply exist through our trial and try to survive it. We must rather learn through it and from it, for God's discipline, or our training to act in accordance with love, does not seem pleasant at the time of experiencing it but for those who are trained by it, peace and righteousness will be their reward (Hebrews 12:11).

This was the same lesson Job had to learn. Though it was a mystery as to why he experienced what he did, he came to learn something profound about himself because of the experience. He says to the Lord,

I know that you can do all things; no plan of yours can be thwarted. You asked, 'Who is this that obscures my counsel without knowledge?' Surely I spoke of things I did not understand, things too wonderful for me to know. You said, 'Listen now, and I will speak; I will question you, and you shall answer me.' My ears had heard of you but now my eyes have seen you. Therefore I despise myself and repent in dust and ashes (Job 42:1-6).

Like Job, we try and reason away why bad things happen to seemingly good people but the truth is we can't. Our perspective, mind, understanding and hearts do not allow for it. What we can do is acknowledge the mystery and lean into the greatness, mercy and power of God. Maybe then, like Job, our view of God and the metaphysical world in general will expand beyond our own vantage point. Maybe then our faculties will move beyond hearing and expand to see God for who he is and therefore acknowledge who we are before an infinite God. Because the person who has turned their disposition back toward God is the one who can say "I despise myself and repent." They have an understanding of who they are as a created being before their creator; as humans before the divine; as dependent on God rather than vice versa, and that nothing is actually deserved in this life but that every breath taken, even if that breath is painful to take, is a precious gift offered graciously by God.

We have much to be thankful for.

"Because of God's great love we are not consumed, for his compassions never fail. They are new every morning; great is your faithfulness" (Lamentations 3:22-23). Without God to sustain us each morning, our life would not exist. Sin and death would consume us. The ancient Jews knew this and therefore had a profoundly different understanding of the problem of evil than modern thinkers do today. They never asked our typical question of "Why do bad things happen to good people" for they had the understanding that all people have gravely sinned and therefore no one is truly good. They therefore rather asked "Why do good things happen to bad people" (Psalm 73; Habakkuk).
Hmm...why do good things happen to bad people?

And they do every single day. It has baffled many minds as to why Paul could write the Thessalonian church to "be joyful always; pray continually; give thanks in all circumstances" (1 Thessalonians 5:16-17). Really? Give thanks in all circumstances? What about the great fear I had when I lost my job? What about the pain I experienced when my girlfriend broke up with me? What about the hurt I had from my parents' divorce? Should I really find joy in those? Should I really give thanks?

Well, it is once again all a matter of perspective. Paul understood that he deserved nothing in this life and therefore everything he experienced was something to be grateful for. His impending death didn't even bring him down because he knew that meant he would be with Christ (Philippians 1:21). Every breath he took, even if it was painful to take, was a breath taken that he did not deserve. Paul understood grace and mercy. Paul understood that God is a very good God.

The difficulty with our understanding of "goodness" is that we apply it only to ourselves. Something is good if it benefits me but if it does not, it must be evil. The Jews, including Paul, had, yet again, a profoundly different understanding of goodness.

God *is* good. God *is* goodness.

The presence and love of God is the greatest goodness humanity will ever experience (Psalm 73) for he is the source of life, love, joy and blessing. All other pleasures and good things are mere shadows of the reality of their source. But they do not have a face. They cannot love you. They cannot give you worth. They cannot seek you out.

And here is what is so beautiful about the mystery of pain and suffering we find ourselves in: God *is* good.

God is present.

God has not left us to struggle alone. It is not as if God was content to sit on a cloud in the sweet by and by and watch his creation kill itself through their choices for self-reign and priority. Our God, unlike any other, took on human form, entered into the chaos, pain, hurt, suffering and sin and put it literally upon his own shoulders. He is not a God who cannot relate to our struggle (Hebrews 4:15) but one who having persevered through our hatred and sin, endured it to the end.

It was our God who was beaten nearly to the point of death.

It was our God who was mocked as a worthless king.

It was our God who took upon his shoulders our cross.

It was our God who had nails driven through his hands and feet.

It was our God who died upon a hill.

It was our God who was silent through it all.

And we are the ones who complain. We are the ones who think our experiences are unjust and unwarranted. We are the ones who think we have to do it alone—who think no one can sympathize with us, carry us, and help us.

Paul reminds us that it is not we who suffer when we experience many trials but it is rather a participation in the suffering that has already taken place. Our suffering, for us who view it as such, is a participation in the death of Christ (Romans 8:17; II Corinthians 1:5) and if we participate in Christ's death, shall we not also participate in his resurrection (Philippians 3:10-11)?

Indeed it shall be so!

This world is not the end of the line. New creation is on the horizon and its first rays have already broken the night sky. Dawn is coming. Christ has risen! There is a day coming when there will be no more death, sorrow, crying or pain; when every tear will be wiped away from our eyes; when the old order of things will pass away (Revelation 21:4).

It will happen. But because it may not happen entirely today should not give us the license to bicker and complain. We should rather ask ourselves how we can instill within others the new creation we have already experienced in ourselves- the Joy that does not run away when our circumstances change. We are those who can say,

> Though the fig tree does not bud
> and there are no grapes on the vines,
> though the olive crop fails
> and the fields produce no food,
> though there are no sheep in the pen
> and no cattle in the stalls,
> yet I will rejoice in the Lord,
> I will be joyful in God my Savior.
>
> The Sovereign Lord is my strength;
> he makes my feet like the feet of a deer,
> he enables me to go on the heights" (Habakkuk 3:17-19).

Life is not found in the circumstances of this world nor in our current condition but in God himself. If God is for us, who, or what can be against us (Romans 8:31)?

For those who are embittered by suffering and remain in their prideful stance, death is the option they are choosing. Lamenting is powerful and necessary but it should never end in resentment for God is always faithful. We all participate in the current chaos of pain and suffering of our world. We all contribute to the pain of all other people because every day we are making choices that affect all other people.

Our duty is not to untangle the mystery. It could never be done. Maybe, if we were to submit to the grace and forgiveness of the God who can see the world from all angles and analyze every heart and admit that we are contributors to the chaos, we would learn to interact in love and be the face of grace, forgiveness and humility to our hurting world.

Maybe then hope would be realized and our world healed.

After all, this is what the dispositional shift away from our sinful nature requires of us. What is beautiful is that when the dispositional shift occurs, it is no longer obligatory but natural. Love will flow from our nature. Love will become the mode by which we live our lives.

So how will you live this day? How will you interact with your neighbor? Will you contribute to the chaos by choosing to prioritize yourself or will you choose to love your neighbor and extend redemption if only for a brief moment but a moment that will equally form your neighbor in a particular way from that moment on?
I hope you will choose the humane way and interact with them in love.

Because in the end, our choices will harden us into one of two types of people: one bent toward God or one bent toward our self; one of which whom we say in the end, "God, your will be done" or one of which whom God says to us, "your will be done."

One is an occupant of God's eternal kingdom (heaven); the other an occupant of their own eternal kingdom (hell).

And when you exist as the only occupant of your own eternal kingdom, you will have a very long and lonely existence.

Because the choice for hell is also the choice for solitude.

Personal reign would have it no other way.

chaptereleven.turningoutward
(theimageofGod)

Because the choice for hell is also the choice for solitude.

Personal reign would have it no other way.

The car sped around the corner as Dan pressed his foot into the gas pedal. He was going eighty-five down a sixty mile per hour highway but he knew he couldn't stop; even though the rain was pounding against his windshield, blurring his vision. Though Meg, his wife, sat in the passenger seat pleading for him to slow down, he had to continue.

In his mind there was no other choice.

Meg's water had broken and this baby was coming.

This was one of the few days Dan had been sober and was for once in his right mind. These days, he managed to eke out a little self-control, maturity and if I dare say, love, to refrain from drinking on the days Meg said she wasn't feeling well or had the feeling that "today might be the day."

But internally, he felt manipulated. Meg had begged for the last week that Dan wouldn't drink so that he would be ready and able to drive her to the hospital when the day came.

Dan began to feel that Meg was telling him she thought it was soon simply to get him to stop drinking. He had always been the manipulator, never the manipulated, and hated having it the other way around. Speeding through the rain, his mind moved to their kitchen earlier that evening.

"Quit lying to me!" Dan had yelled as he pushed Meg against the refrigerator door. "You keep saying you are having this child and it never comes! Do you want me to stop drinking? Is that what you want?"

Dan took a bottle off the counter and threw it against the kitchen wall behind him. Beer ran down the splotchy, white wall and puddled on the floor.

Dan's arms were firmly grasped to Meg's shoulders and he shook her back and forth, her head hitting the freezer compartment above the fridge behind her. With every shove, Meg's knees became weaker and less stable.

"Damn it, Meg. You think you are so damn smart pulling me around with your lies! You want me to stop drinking? You want me to be a different man? You want someone else? You think I won't be a good father?!"

All Meg could do was whisper "No" through silent tears. But Dan had heard enough. He didn't care what her response was. With that, he shoved her away. But her legs could no longer support her. Weakened, she fell face-down, sobbing in front of the refrigerator.

Once upon a time, humanity was very much like a child inside of its mother's womb. The connection between a mother and child in-utero is inexplicable. When my wife was pregnant with our son, I watched as *storge* blossomed within her as he grew inside her. The connection they shared was like none other on earth. He shared her body. What she ate, he ate; what she drank, he drank. The air she breathed affected him. She couldn't take certain medicines because everything that entered her body was filtered through him. Our son was entirely dependent upon her for every need he had while developing in the womb.

Our son's dependence on my wife was not limited to his physical existence either. While in birthing class, we were told to talk with our son regularly, read to him, surround him with music, and pray for him. They said that the more human interaction a child has inside the womb, the better developed the child would be socially and communally. More importantly, they told us to touch our child–to connect physically with our child and to even begin playing with him. Touch, they said, is one of the greatest forms of care a child can receive.

With this in mind, we took every opportunity to care for him in this way.

If there was a bump from an elbow, a knee or a fist, we would touch him, rub him and tell him how excited we were to finally meet him face to face. We would sing songs to him, pray for him, talk with him about random everyday things. We took that proof and followed it to the letter.

My son's life force, in every way, was entirely outside of himself. Without a mother to carry him, he would have died. Without both of us to love him, speak to him, sing to him, touch him, play with him and care for him, his humanity would not have been fully known or realized.

Being known by someone else is a key part of what it means to be human. In other words, intimacy is necessary for survival. But mere survival is not the end of life as evolutionists would have us believe. Intimacy is necessary for something greater: living. To know and to be known in relationship is at the very foundation of meaningful human existence.

And this not just for a child inside its mother's womb; this is the case for all of humanity.

The need for intimacy transcends age, gender, class, race, time and proximity. Wherever and whoever you are, the fact that you are human means you are a relational being longing to know another and to be known.

You need intimacy. Your very humanity requires it.

Once humanity had reliance upon a life force—the only life force—outside of itself, namely God. Intimacy was woven into the fabric of their being. The Bible describes this connection as being created in the "Image of God" (Genesis 1:27). Somehow, being God's image bearers provides us our humanity. Somehow, we are intimately connected to God through his image.

The problem with intimacy is that it necessitates reliance on something outside of ourselves. But due to our self-reign, we no longer acknowledge that our humanity is reliant on God. Notice how this plays out in the story or Adam and Eve.

Intimacy is bound in agape love. But if Adam and Eve were to submit to agape, they could not at the same time submit to themselves. And so they were left at a fork in the road. Would they continue to live in intimate connection with God their creator? Or should they forgo intimacy with God and one another and declare themselves rulers?

As we know, they chose the latter.

They, and therefore all of humanity along with them, took their intimate connection with God, unplugged it, and plugged it into themselves. Thus, the sinful nature is merely a manipulation of the more basic nature that has always existed. The sinful nature did not create anything new within humanity; it simply manipulated what was already there.

Because of this, Genesis tells us that God banished Adam and Eve from the Garden and his presence and he placed an angel with a flaming sword at its entrance so they could not come back in to eat from the tree of life and live forever and without hope in their depraved state (3:23-24).

And for thousands of years, no one saw God.

Some saw his back (Exodus 33:23) and even that was more than they could bear (Exodus 34:30) but his face was always hidden.

But again, it is not as if some great divide fell between man and God but rather humanity was no longer holy. They were no longer set apart for God in intimate connection with him but rather set on their own thoughts, desires and will. The face of God, even if they desired to see it, would be unbearable—it would have killed them.

So much was the case that the Levitical priests, before entering God's presence in the Holy of Holies on the Day of Atonement needed to fully cleanse and purify themselves from all sin because if this were not the case, the holiness and presence of God would kill them instantly. They therefore tied ropes around their legs so that if it were the case that the holiness of God killed them in their sin, someone could pull them out and retrieve their body (Leviticus 16:1-2).

God's holiness has always been greater than our sin.

And thanks be to God that his holiness condemns our sin. That he was not content to let us remain where we were: disconnected.

That he pursued us.

Long ago, Adam and Eve broke that intimate connection between us and our Creator. Although it was severed, it was not fully lost. We are not

Life and Love and Why

without hope because God's image is, at least in part, still within us. The difficulty is that many have scraped, clawed and torn against this intimacy to the point that very little of it remains: it has been buried, beaten and destroyed to the point of almost non-existence.

But what is beautiful is that our intimate connection to God does still remain. It can never, on this side of eternity, be fully destroyed. John Calvin knew that all people, by the mere fact that they are human, have a general knowledge of God. Paul too understood that God has made knowledge about himself plain to humanity: "For since the creation of the world God's invisible qualities—his eternal power and divine nature—have been clearly seen, being understood from what has been made, so that men are without excuse" (Romans 1:19-20).

We must acknowledge that this connection is not just a façade or only present whenever it is convenient for us. God resides within every one of us because we bear his image.

We are, after all, still human.

Meg's water broke on impact as her stomach hit the kitchen floor. All she could do was lay there—her legs would no longer support her. If she were honest with herself, she didn't really want to move. The sight of Dan standing over her broke what was left of her will and ambition.

But as Dan looked down at Meg lying in amniotic fluid and tears and saw the distressed look on her face, a particular memory came to mind. He remembered, for the first time in over half a decade, the sound of a woman's voice muffled under his hand against her mouth, a woman he had known for only a brief moment, but a woman he had hurt—and then killed. He remembered the pain he experienced as he watched her writhing as he forced himself on-top of her. He remembered shoving that pain deeper and deeper into non-existence so he could do what he had determined he was going to do.

But this time was different.

Meg had a face. She wasn't an object or a random girl who he saw through drunken eyes as a toy for his pleasure or abuse. She was Meg. Dan knew her. They lived life together. They sometimes laughed together.

They sometimes cried together.

And so he knelt down next to Meg, fought through her defensive right arm swinging weakly at his embrace, picked her up, carried her to his car, locked her in and sped away to the hospital.

The rhythm of the pounding rain against the windshield put Dan into deep contemplation regarding what had taken place over the last half hour and the last twenty-five years of his life.

"What am I doing?" He said to himself as his pace had now calmed as the traffic got thicker. "I can't bring a child into this world. I can't raise this baby. I don't know the first damn thing about raising a baby."

The hospital was now in view and Dan's anxiety increased. Contemplating how his own mother and father neglected him helped very little in providing him insight into raising children. It only made him more scared of the situation in front of him.

He never wanted to be like them. But as he looked at himself in the rear-view mirror, all he saw was them in his eyes.

He had become what he hated.

He may not have sold anyone's possessions for gambling money but there were many people in his life that he should have paid more attention to but didn't. There were many who he emotionally abused, considered worthless and a burden. These were the same messages he was taught about himself. He was a mistake and he knew it. It was the clearest message his parents ever communicated to him: "You are such a burden...If that is the way you are going to act, you can leave and sleep on the streets...You are worthless...You're such a pain...Could you be any more bothersome? Let me be.

Nothing good will ever come from you." And Dan believed it.

But what kept going through Dan's mind as he sat at the red light across from the hospital was if it had to be the same for his child? Did he have to be his parents? Did he have to communicate to his child what his parents communicated to him? Would his child have to grow up like he did? Would his child think it had the same worthless qualities he did about himself? Would it be loved? Would it receive his essence?

It was common in ancient Judaic thought to assume that children would inherit the nature of their parents. They held this so firmly that they believed they could point out a drunkard or adulterer because their image would be stamped on their children. Or in other words, the children, through their behavior, would portray the true nature of their parents.

Now, it may be true that if a parent smokes or drinks regularly, has promiscuous relations outside of marriage or gets divorced, that their children are more likely to do the same. But children are not just mounds of clay that we can shape, mold and bend into whoever we desire. They themselves are independent human beings. While they do require instruction, they still have a choice as to who they become. But we do not live in a vacuum. What we do and say will assist in forming them into who they will be.

On a much wider scale, however, the general principle is true of all of us: we have all inherited the nature of our first parents, Adam and Eve. But remember that my father's sinful nature might not look the same in me as it does in him. This does not mean it is different; both our natures are directed toward self-reign, self-preservation and self-priority. It may be manifested differently, but both natures are equally sinful.

What differentiates us from Adam and Eve is that they had a choice in the matter as to what nature they proclaimed as their own. They were made in God's image, likeness and holiness (Genesis 5:1) but their son, Seth, was not (Genesis 5:3). Seth inherited, as we all have, the sin of his mother and father.

He got what was given to him.

Because he was made in the image of Adam (Genesis 5:3).

And Enosh was made in the image of Seth (Genesis 5:6).

And Kenan was made in the image of Enosh (Genesis 5:9).

And Mahalalel was made in the image of Kenan (Genesis 5:12).

The line and pattern continues to you and me. Only Adam and Eve were *created* in the image of God. Everyone after them was created in the image of their father and mother. We have inherited their essence.

The ancient Jews understood that being *created* in the image of God meant being indwelled with and defined by his essence. The image upon the first humans was God's own nature indwelling them. Considering that God is love, this means their lives were directed towards love in a reciprocating fashion with one another and with God.

As God is love, so were Adam and Eve.

The two creation stories in Genesis (chapters 1 and 2) lead us to believe that the indwelling of God's image was the breath of God indwelling Adam's nostrils and lungs. The Jews also believed that the breath of God was the very soul within the human person. It was this which separated humans from trees, water, animals and all other created things. And it was at the point when God's breathe entered humanity that they became "living beings" (Genesis 2:7).

It was because of this that they were declared "very good" (Genesis 1:31) and were set apart from the rest of creation. It was God's breath residing within Adam's lungs that made him human—a living being. We too are human because God's breath still resides within ours.

God's image remains, though only in part, in every one of us.

We are, after all, still human.

Life and Love and Why

Because Meg's fall had initiated her water breaking, she was immediately admitted to labor and delivery for monitoring and examination. It was quickly determined that a c-section delivery would be safest.
Dan couldn't bring himself to be present during the surgery for he knew and acknowledged he was the one who put her there. He rather paced back and forth in the waiting room coping with the silence of several others in waiting, the blue speckled carpet, white walls and sterility of smell, sound and site.

He knew he had done a lot of bad things in his life but the events of this day had, for the first time, drove him to try and understand why he did what he did in his past and also who he had become.

For the first time, he felt remorse.

The surgery didn't take long and therefore Dan was surprised when the nurse came to get him from the waiting room. He wasn't ready to see his child. He was still too scared to be a father. He wasn't ready to face Meg and look her in the eyes and see the hurt he had caused her. He would have preferred more preparation time, more time to think. More time to figure out what to say to Meg. He had never even held a baby before. He had only seen one from a distance or in a magazine. What do you say to a new born? How do you hold it? How do you care for it?

How do you love it?

Dan walked slowly to the operation room where Meg and his newborn baby were. He prepped himself, as the sign commanded, pushed through the door and for the first time, saw his baby: a girl. They named her Leila, for she was beautiful. Dan had never seen such blue eyes, perfect skin and pure innocence.

He thought to himself for one of the few times in as long as he could remember, "There is good in this world.

She is beautiful in every way."

Life and Love and Why

Being human means having at least a remnant of the divine within us which is what gives us our humanity. But even more, the remnant that remains is the very love of God, his agape. Our humanity is bound up in God's reciprocating love nature: we are human because God loves us. Our life is sustained only because we are connected to God in an intimate way. Because his breath infiltrates our lungs, we have the very power to breathe. The moment we die is the moment we are no longer connected to God. It is the moment his breath is taken away.

The ancient Jews believed that the name of God could not be said, not because saying it was against some rule somewhere (although the third commandment does speak against the abuse of God's name) but because the human tongue literally did not have the capacity to pronounce it. They understood that God's name was pronounced through the sounds and action of breathing.

With every breath we take, we are saying God's name.

YHWH. YHWH.. YHWH... YHWH.... YHWH.....

Thus, life began when an infant said God's name—took its first breath—and ended when that ability ceased.

This belief should not give us grounds for accepting abortion, however. A child inside of its mother's womb is equally human because that child, even at conception, shares the life sustaining breath of its mother.

God's life sustains the life of the child as it does its mother. God provides both their humanity.

The two are always interconnected. Always intimate.

Therefore, all people are of invaluable worth because our worth is tied up in our being human. The child in India, who was born with AIDS, put into an orphanage and may be one of the twenty-five thousand children who starve to death every day, has the same worth as the dictator of Zibabwe who prevents that child from receiving aide. Both are human. Both are of great worth.

The man who, because of fighting in a war and having experienced the pain, hatred, bitterness and fear that come along with it, now sleeps under a bridge in a worn-out sleeping bag he pulled from a dumpster, feeds off of other people's trash and a few people's generosity and really has no interest in talking with anyone other than himself has the same worth as the wealthy business man who grew up in a city suburb, sleeps in a cushiony bed in his own room within his own house, eats whatever he desires for every meal of every day and has the latest and best cell phone and webcam to talk with the most important people he knows. Both are human. Both are of great worth.

God provides us our worth, not our circumstances, the world, or its people. But living into our worth and therefore being *fully* human means to have intimate connection with the source of our humanity.

Adam and Eve were originally the true representatives of what it meant to be human. The fullness of God resided with them and therefore their nature was the true nature of humanity. Their decision to abandon that nature, however, left their humanity tainted. Once they sinned, their humanity became corrupted and deficient.

What, then, has become apparent is that in order to become intimate with the source of humanity (that is, God), we need a new humanity that has not been tainted by the choice for sin. The Bible's cry for a new birth is not to be one in the physical sense, as Nicodemus thought (John 3:4), but a spiritual one (I Corinthians 15:42). In the first century Roman political context, one could only attain Roman citizenship through birth, that is, only by being born in the Roman Empire. Citizenship could not be bought or gained. So it is with the Kingdom of God: as flesh gives birth to flesh, so the Spirit gives birth to Spirit (John 3:6).

So how are we to go about doing this? Since Adam, the "living being" has apparently ruined humanity, how then are we to reconnect with our source, to turn around? In I Corinthians 15, Paul talks about the second Adam who came to help us re-attain the nature the first Adam lost. But because of our sinful nature, the second Adam could not assist us in reclaiming God's image unless he was from God himself.

Enter Jesus Christ (John 1:1, 14).

Jesus did not inherit the essence of his earthly parents because his incarnation was through the Holy Spirit (Matthew 1:18). Jesus, in other words, was not *made* in the image of God but *is* himself the image of God (II Corinthians 4:4; Colossians 1:15). He is the true provider of humanity because his humanity lacks nothing.

Our goal then is to reclaim the full image of God in Jesus Christ and have his breath infiltrate not only our nostrils or our lungs but the entirety of who we are. We must reclaim his essence by the re-birth of our Spirits. Our natures must turn around. We need to experience a dispositional shift. We then shall be declared as God's offspring and children of His Spirit and therefore "live, move and have our being" in he and he alone (Acts 17:28).

The God who is love will define us.

When he does, new creation of our spiritual being takes shape. Jesus Christ is the fullest example of what it means to be human. We are therefore most human when we imitate him. By being bound to Jesus Christ (who is the perfect image of God) including his life, death and resurrection we will be a new creation.

The old has gone, the new has come (II Corinthians 5:17)!

Once we reclaim the image of God in Jesus Christ for ourselves, our lives are redirected toward love for God and for one another. We live how we were always meant to live.

Our call, then, is to live out of our great value as redeemed people, bent not towards ourselves but to God in love, to instill within others great value. Because we have reclaimed the fullness of humanity does not give us license to rule over others who have not. All people have immeasurable worth because they are indwelled with a remnant of God's essence. So, how we treat them is how we treat the God within them.

When we are bound in love, we are called to serve.

Our "greater" value does not allow us to look down on others but demands we bend down to lift others up.

Life and Love and Why

chaptertwelve.love'sreflection
(church)

Our "greater" value does not allow us to look down on others but demands we bend down to lift others up.

"Go away! Please, leave. Please, please, please..." Dan's voice echoed against the cinder block walls of his four by six foot solitary confinement cell. He was on his fourth month of being alone; but he didn't know this. He could no longer differentiate minutes from hours; days from months. The only human interaction he had was when the guard silently took him to work out, also in isolation, for one hour a day and when receiving his food through a two by six inch slit in his door. The effects of being alone were causing him to suffer from intense hallucinations.

He couldn't sleep more than two hours at a time and usually his sleep only lasted fifteen minutes. He spent most of his time pacing back and forth counting in his head the number of steps he took. "One, two, three," pivot, "four, five, six," pivot, "seven, eight, nine," pivot..." By the time he reached two-thousand steps, his heals were worn down, blistered and bleeding. When he could no longer walk, he spent his time rocking back and forth talking to imaginary friends who sometimes, by Dan's conversation, seemed more like enemies and listening to music that didn't actually exist. He could no longer separate reality from imagination. When the music wouldn't stop and his "friends" wouldn't leave, he repeatedly slammed his head against the wall until the blood from the gash in his forehead he made blinded his already dim vision.

He blacked out.

He never experienced the human interaction from the prison nurses who came in to minister to his wounds. They were gone by the time he awoke. "Am I alive?" He wondered as he pressed his fingers into his cheeks. *He honestly wasn't sure. He could no longer feel anything. "What have I done to deserve this?! I can't do this anymore!"* He screamed but the echoes muffled any comprehension of what he said.

"Please...please...somebody kill me." The lights went out and deepest blackness filled the air as Dan shrunk into the corner, wrapped his arms around his legs, folded his head into his knees and cried himself to sleep.

We were never meant to be alone in this world. Remember, intimacy is part of what makes us human. God, after he had created Adam, said "It is not good for the man to be alone. I will make a helper suitable for him" (Genesis 2:18). And so God caused Adam to fall into a deep sleep. While asleep, God took from Adam a single rib and from this rib, he created Eve, meaning "life."

In the cultures surrounding Israel at the time this creation poem was written, the word "rib," or *Ti*, also meant "life." Essentially, "from life, God creates life." There is equality within creation, not sexist hierarchy as some have suggested. On the contrary, Adam lacked something within his personhood that required a counterpart. He could not fully function within himself. He needed Eve.

Or rather, he needed community.

Outside of community, we are deficient within our personhood, our humanity and ourselves.

As the 17th century poet John Donne observed, "No man [or woman] is an island, entire of itself."[xx] All find their full humanity only when they exist within community.

As we discussed earlier, we find our meaning through the image of God in Jesus Christ. If our humanity finds its source in the breath of God and his image indwelling us, then our humanity is naturally communal.

God is communal. God is triune.

The Bible never explicitly claims that God is Trinity and yet this claim is at the very foundation of Christian theology. But the theology of a Trinitarian God has also been the source of much confusion and debate. The paradox of three in oneness just doesn't make sense to some, and for many, if Scriptural support is not verbatim, it is not authoritative. The philosophy and theology of the trinity is an interesting discussion, some might say, but because there is no church-wide consensus, we can't really land on anything definitive about it.

Even if this is true, it shouldn't stop us from trying to understand it. The trinity is not only important as a theological construct but more so because in the Trinitarian God rests our life, our love and the meaning of everything.

Let's take the premise that God is agape love (I John 4:8, 16). If God is love, God, by love's definition, must be other-oriented. Thus, because God is infinite and immutable (he does not change), he has been love even prior to the creation of humanity. God must then exist as a plurality of persons because God's creation, considering it had not yet been created, could not be the sole object of his love by the very definition of his existence (i.e. agape). But why trinity? Why not duality?

I am finite. Because this is the case, I cannot extend my agape love to multiple parties at the same time. This is what is known as the "law of beneficence." I only have so much to give and can only give it within the time and space my finite existence allows me. The other loves (phileo, storge and eros), on the other hand, can be provided to multiple parties only because these loves are not sacrificial in nature. Whatever is sacrificial about them is the remnant of agape that exists within them. The love I have for my son, for example, will not diminish when I have, Lord willing, a second child. Storge allows for the expansion of itself to multiple parties. However, true Agape, is active and giving and because our finiteness, by definition, means we are limited, agape cannot be distributed continuously without exhaustion and to multiple parties.

Our finiteness is in part why Jesus tells us we must "love our neighbor as our self" (Matthew 22:39). We must know we are loved in order to love. Without the love of self, we cannot fully love our neighbor; we would have nothing to give them. The Christian life is not one of perpetually draining love and then "retreating" to be filled again. This would be the promotion of a compartmentalized Christian faith. Because of our finiteness, God, as the source of love, fills us with his love, which we then in turn extend to others. To love the self then is to first know that we are loved, and then out of that knowledge, extend that love to others.

Our task is to grow in our ability to do this within our capacity to move in space and time. We are limited. But what if I were above space and time? What if I were infinite? What if my love had no end? What if I could give of myself without limitation to billions of people and still be full within myself? What if I were God?

What if I were triune?

Trinity has no boundaries. God is infinite; he cannot fit into a box, he can give of himself to multiple parties without deficiency and he is not limited in the extension of his love? He is a dynamic force, living and breathing, active and speaking; he is not a static God with his arms crossed unable or unwilling to interact with our world.

God is Triune. He can prove himself as love to multiple parties, not to mention billions of individuals without mitigating the love within his own personhood. God is a trinity because he is infinite reciprocal love relationship within himself. Out of this love and essence, then, he created humanity in his image.

His infinite love could not be contained:

"So God *created man* in his own image, in the image of God he *created him*; male and female he *created them*" (Genesis 1:27). The poetic nature of the creation story informs us that the creation of the first human persons was a triune achievement and upon the inclusion of the infinite, reciprocating and triune God (the third stanza) humanity became communal: whole.

Father creates.

Son creates.

Spirit creates.

Because God chose to create in his image (i.e. that of endless reciprocating love), it was necessary that he create more than one human being.

As God is communal, so is humanity.

So when we are absent from community—the ability to reciprocate love in relationship—our humanity is diminished. We are not living out of God's being which enables our humanity. The beautiful paradox is how God creating humanity as a single individual promotes the community of all human persons. The ancient Jewish rabbis understood that God created the human race as a single individual (Adam) because they believed what is done to a single person is done to the entire human race. Whoever therefore destroys one life, destroys the entire world and likewise, whoever saves one life, saves the entire world.

Our actions always have communal implications. We all affect one another. We are all interconnected. Your humanity is intimately tied to my humanity. All lives inform and shape one another. Just as your life informs mine, so all deaths diminish us because we all are connected to one another and we together make up the human race.

I hope this would make us mourn greater for the atrocities we see on the news or experience on our streets and perhaps be more earnest about ridding our lives of participating in them. I hope it would allow us to celebrate more exuberantly when victories are won and injustice defeated. Our humanity is bound up in one another and when one person is not living full into their humanity, it creates a leak in all other people's potential to do so. We are most human together, not apart. When one is humiliated, all are. When one is oppressed, all are.

Understanding this connection to all humanity is crucial for those earnest in following the Christian life. To call oneself a Christ-follower in our human finiteness is to do what God did in his infiniteness—serve others diligently and passionately out of love.

If we want to be bound in love, we must necessarily be bound in community. Love requires it; love is communal. Just as God does not exist as an isolated individual, neither can those who claim to follow him. We need others to extend our love to and also to receive it from.

When this is done in a reciprocating fashion, it is what the New Testament calls the church. Luke describes it this way:

> All the believers were together and had everything in common. Selling their possessions and goods, they gave to anyone as they had need...All the believers were one in heart and mind. No one claimed that any of their possessions was their own, but they shared everything they had...There were no needy persons among them. For from time to time those who owned the lands or houses sold them, brought the money from the sales and put it at the apostles'

feet, and it was distributed to anyone as they had need (Acts 2:44-45; 4:32-34).

What Luke is describing is a community so tightly bound in love that *koinonia* ("fellowship") naturally takes place, a community where humanity is drawn together in unity. Koinonia exists where the needs of a single individual are met by the agape among the whole body of covenant members. The need of one becomes the need of all. The hurts of an individual unit become the hurts of the community, and the one is lifted upon the shoulders of the many. It is also a community where the celebrations are shared not in envy or covetousness, but in true joy and appreciation, both with the recipient and with God.

It is a different model of church than I grew up with. It is a different model of church than what I typically see. We often speak of "community" as place-oriented. We have our neighborhoods, our schools, our cities. Our "church community" is the people who show up to a particular building on Sunday mornings. We hardly ever see that the only thing shared between believers is the building with a cross on top.

But community is not two or more people in close proximity. Proximity is important only to establish availability and regularity within the body. Community is rather the giving and receiving of love in covenant relationship. Unfortunately, our communities are more often than not void of covenant and therefore only exist as shadows of a deeper community. Covenant is what binds one person to another. It is the intentional decision and communal agreement to abandon the flesh and its interests for the benefit others. This is precisely why God is the purest form of community. And it is also why Jesus prays to his father that we would be "one, just as you are in me and I am in you" (John 17:21). Have you ever thought about how united Jesus is with his Father? Jesus' hope was that his followers would be the same way. His vision for the church was that they would exist as Trinitarian communities. In the same way God reciprocates love within himself our churches would do the same.

Like God, when love is reciprocated, it cannot be contained. Reciprocating love exists to reach out and bring others into it. There ought not to be need within the church community or the external communities in close proximity because the many should support the few.

However, what typically takes place in churches, unfortunately, is that the few support the many. But rather than the resources of the few going to the actual needs of the many, they are largely funneled into a budget that exists to support an infrastructure, an electric bill and a multi-media ritual seen only on Sunday mornings when the church opens its doors to the light of day. If the building supports the development of true reciprocating fellowship and love, it might be justified but all things that don't lead to a greater development and understanding of agape love within community are done in vain.

And the devil loves it.

The church is supposed to be the body of Christ (Ephesians 5:23; Colossians 1:24). The church was meant to be the manifestation of Christ to our world. It is simply unfortunate that this vision has largely gotten lost within our business plans, marketing endeavors, corporate structures and search for cultural relevance. Have we abandoned God's law and conformed to the standards of the nations around us (Ezekiel 11:12)?

It wouldn't be the first time.

A body is living, breathing, active, moving, and growing. But we have always understood the church to be a noun. Isn't the church a place? A thing? A people?

Of course, the church is the people. But it adds very little to the overall discussion to say "The church is the people," not the building. I think most of us have already come to that conclusion.

But is this sufficient?

Yea, the church is the people, we get that. But the church is only the people if those people are living a certain way. The church is therefore not the bodies in close proximity that make up a people but the intricate, intentional movement of those people as they learn what it means to follow Christ with every effort of their lives.

In other words, church is a verb.

And this doesn't even require a building.

The church is movement. It is the outpouring of reciprocating love as people live in relationship and life is shared in Trinitarian community. The church exists and functions as the active embodiment of the Godhead giving and receiving love to proclaim that sin and personal reign have been defeated. Life has been found—our image reclaimed. If this is not happening within the building we call the church, church is not taking place.

After all, the purpose of meeting together is to spur one another on towards love and good deeds (Hebrews 10:24-25). If we are the body of Christ, we are the healing and redemptive agent to a broken and hurting world.

I would hope we don't remain content with self-centered, internally driven "community." The world needs us. The point of discipleship is not to puff ourselves up but to reach out in love to build others up (1 Corinthians 8:1).

If love is contained, it is not real.

Remember, agape, by its very definition is outward focused.

True Trinitarian community is always active and taking shape as a body learning what it means to love one another as God has loved them (John 15:12).

When this happens in community, sin is constantly purged because as our ability and capacity to love grows, sin naturally deflates for sin too, like love, is communal.

chapterthirteen.thefaceoftruthingrace
(rebuke)

When this happens in community, sin is constantly purged because as our ability and capacity to love grows, sin naturally deflates for sin too, like love, is communal.

As we have established in the previous chapters, sin is relational. If sin is the expression of my self-reign and priority over another person, there must be another person, at least in thought, for me to reign over—and yes, that person can be God.

But what happens when "me" becomes "us?" What happens when true, Trinitarian community is formed? What happens when a marriage takes place (the appropriation of Trinitarian community; i.e. people bound together in covenant)? Consider Adam and Eve. We are told that they became husband and wife (Genesis 2:25) and thereby became "one flesh" (Genesis 2:24). Now, one's actions directly affect the other and they thereby become responsible for one another's sins.

We see this with the first one. Both Adam and Eve stood before the serpent and heard his lies. Both recalled God's clear command. Both chose to eat.

The birth of the sinful nature was a communal attainment. When Adam and Eve chose to reign over God and eat of the fruit of the tree of knowledge and good and evil, the effect of their choice only came when both ate of it: an intentional act of rebellion against the clear command God had given them. "When the woman saw that the tree was good for food and pleasing to the eye, and also desirable for gaining wisdom, she took some and ate it. She also gave some to her husband, who was with her, and he ate it. Then the eyes of both of them were opened..." (Genesis 3:6-7).

The eating of the tree was the solidifying of something deep within them. It was the hardening of their desire to reign over God and over one another. It was the turning of their backs on God.

If only one of them would have chosen to eat of the fruit, however, the sinful nature would not have been planted. Sin requires a counterpart. Eve could not have ruled over Adam if Adam was still identified with God. She could try to rule over him, but only in the confines of her own mind. She therefore would have probably gone insane, because being thus separated from Adam, she would no longer be able to be in community with him, and thus deny her own humanity.

Eventually she would have died while Adam would continue to live.

Life would have once again had to be taken from life.

Sure, this is speculative, but the point is because both sinned, the suppression of each other and therefore the reign over each other was able to grow and foster into hatred, division, oppression, domination, tyranny, cruelty, coercion, manipulation, dissension and all other faces of pain, suffering and self-reign in our world. Moreover, because they both participated, they passed this hellish gift on to their children.

We have become what they were. Our hearts too are bent inward upon ourselves rather than outward in love for another.

Thus, we that have reoriented our hearts toward love have a great responsibility. One of the missions of the Trinitarian community is to be the light to the world (Matthew 5:14), drawing all people into it. We are to be a community bound in love: the current manifestation of God's kingdom and he made known to all people. Our calling is to be a people whose hearts are bent back towards God in love, turned around facing him, and to help all others who come into community do the same.

The point is not to merely point our fingers and condemn the outsider but to bring them to an understanding of who they are without God, without Love (selfish human beings bent inwards on themselves). Through our love, we are to extend grace, mercy, forgiveness and compassion, just as Christ (the human embodiment of the Trinity) did for us.

If we only indoctrinate them to our church principles and rules, they will be no better off in the end than they were when they entered community. All we have done is simply padded the wide road to destruction for them. We would have given them hope in salvation and a picture of their own utopian paradise, an arena where they are still king, ruler and authority. If this is the case, we have only given them a cheerful and appealing picture of hell.

If our motivation as Christians seeking maturity in Christ is to sin less and simply abide by some list of church rules, we are sorely far off the path.

The correction of our nature is such that it will never be enough to look at less pornography or to gossip less or to stop having promiscuous relationships. Sin transcends behavior and *doing*. Sin is about the way you view the world and the people around you. It is about you in relationship with all people and how you view yourself in light of them.

Sin is communal in the sense that it necessitates more than one party be involved—even if one of the parties involved is passively so. Just as love is the binding force for community, sin is the shattering force in community. Self-reign proclaims that my life revolves around *me*, while love proclaims that my life revolves around *us*.

Do you see the difference?

The person bent toward sin cannot also be bent towards love—community. They may participate in "place-community" and may be devout church attendees, but their involvement in community is only skin deep. There is no covenant. This does not necessarily mean they don't have real relationships. But because their relationships are inherently outside of God in agape based community, their relationship cannot give them life. The community they know is a mere caricature. It can only provide a shadow of the authentic life that can be found in the Triune God.

But is this what the church has become? Have we become a bunch of individuals wearing masks that look like Jesus but are really only hiding the selfish ambition and vain conceit that are revealed when we leave the church doors and take the masks off? Has this Christianity thing just become a "part" of our lives? Are we just seeking a good "balance" of our spiritual lives and our secular lives? Have we only become a consumer of the kingdom of God rather than an active participant and citizen of it?

Is this church thing something I only do on Sundays?
Or does the covenant based, love community of the Trinitarian God define who I am?

Because if my individual priorities are still intact when I enter into covenant community, I am the death of that community. And if I persist in claiming priority while in this community, I am also the face of death to the others within it. This is because sin is a communal problem. What you do does not only affect you but all others within your community. If self-reign is allowed to foster within our community, your sin becomes my sin, and vice versa.

A good example of this is found in the Old Testament book of Joshua. After the defeat of Jericho, an individual by the name of Achan chose to keep some of the spoils of the city for himself, something God had forbidden the Israelite soldiers to do. As a result, God's "anger burned against Israel" (Joshua 7:1). Consequently, this one man's sin caused the defeat of the Israelite army at Ai, a small pastoral community with hardly any military expertise. When Joshua cries out to God hoping for an answer as to why his people fell in battle, God does not say Achan is to blame, but all of Israel: "Israel has sinned; they have violated my covenant, which I commanded them to keep. They have taken some of the devoted things; they have stolen, they have lied, they have put them with their own possessions. That is why the Israelites cannot stand against their enemies" (Joshua 7:11).

Sin always involves more than one party. As a result of Achan's sin, not only was the Israelite army defeated in battle, but as punishment, both Achan and all his family were stoned to death (Joshua 7:24-26).

Covenant, although grace based, still demands justice.

We are all interconnected. Our humanity is bound up in one another. Your sin affects me as mine affects you. The Jewish Rabbi's told this parable to illustrate this fact:

> It is like a company of men on board a ship. One of them took a drill and began to bore a hole under him. The other passengers said to him, "What are you doing?" He replied, "What has that to do with you? Am I not making the hole under my seat?" They retorted, "But the water will enter and drown us all!"[xxi]

Our choices to sin are not just our own choices for death. If our sin is brought into the community, the community will wither. When beautiful flower beds become overgrown by weeds, the flowers are choked of their resources and eventually die. If we are passive in dealing with the sins of the individuals within our community, their choice for death will affect how our community functions.

When our passivity to speak into their life allows them to remain in death, we are equally unloving. When we are passive in love, we are active in anti-love. Or if you remember, active in sin and although their guilt might not fall on my shoulders, the responsibility of their choices does.

Rebuke, albeit hard to do, is therefore necessary for health and growth to take place. Even the great prophet Ezekiel had to be reminded of this:

> When I [God] say to a wicked man, 'You will surely die,' and you do not warn him or speak out to dissuade him from his evil ways in order to save his life, that wicked man will die for his sin, and I will hold you accountable for his blood. But if you do warn the wicked man and he does not turn from his wickedness or from his evil ways, he will die for his sin; but you will have saved yourself. Again, when a righteous man turns from his righteousness and does evil, and I put a stumbling block before him, he will die. Since you did not warn him, he will die for his sin. The righteous things he did will not be remembered, and I will hold you accountable for his blood. But if you do warn the righteous man not to sin and he does not sin, he will surely live because he took warning, and you will have saved yourself (Ezekiel 3:18-21).

"Really?" we say. "It seems a bit harsh. Being passive towards a brother or sister in my community has never been on any of the sin lists I saw growing up. In fact, I thought we were supposed to turn away when we saw people doing things we knew they shouldn't be. I thought it more appropriate to talk to everyone else I knew about their sin than talk with them directly.

That would just be awkward.

Let their sin be their sin, and I will deal with my own. Let's not make this community thing messier than we have to."

It is precisely this mentality that caused the ruin of entire cities and people groups in the Old Testament. As Moses and Aaron asked after Korah had sinned, "O God, God of the spirits of all mankind, will you be angry with the entire assembly when only one man sins" (Numbers 16:22)?

The answer is always yes. Look back at the story of Achan. That sin is a personal, private affair is a blatant lie of the devil. Entire nations were guilty of an individual's sin simply because there was no one willing to confront the sin, rebuke an individual and lead them out of death. The prophets tried time and time again but with little avail. The prophets would be saved by their righteousness (Ezekiel 14:14) but the nations who killed them would not. The individual's sinful choices therefore became the death of the many (e.i. Amos 7:10-17). If I acknowledge sin in my community and yet fail to rid the community of it, I become a participant in the sin.

Acknowledging the sin, however, is only a small part of the battle. Fighting anti-love requires action. You either actively love and speak against the sin that leads to death or you actively hate and allow for your brother or sister to remain in their death.

Every day we watch our friends and family dig their own graves and we stand by allowing them to continue. Sooner or later they are going to finish, put down their shovel and crawl in.

At what point do we say, "enough"?

We have a great responsibility as redeemed people to illustrate the great love of God for all people through Trinitarian community. But love is not this fluffy-teddy-bear-stuffed-message that we enclose in a heart and timidly slide into our crush's locker.

Love is a blood soaked cross bearing down upon your shoulders. Love is offensive for it tells you that in your natural predisposition, you are dead and in the wrong, something no one wants to hear. But it is the only thing that will bring you out of death and wake you up to the greater human existence waiting for you if you would only humble yourself, take up your cross and follow Christ. To the person who has neglected and shunned love their whole life by living only for themselves, love is the most frightening and painful thing they may ever experience. It is and will be their judge (James 2:12). And why would we ever assume purging would feel good? Scraping the dead away from the heart still requires that the chest be opened up. Love is painful in the same way cutting away a cancerous growth is painful. But without the necessary operation, the growth will kill its carrier.

Your sinful nature will kill you—in more ways than you know—if it is not dealt with.

Our task, then, is evangelistic. If Christ is the hope of the world and we are those who are in him, are we too not the hope of the world? "How beautiful on the mountains are the feet of those who bring good news, who proclaim peace, who bring good tidings, who proclaim salvation, who say to Zion, 'Your God reigns'" (Isaiah 52:7)! The point of our evangelistic efforts needs to be to bring people to a redeemed state where they can say, "God you reign over my life, I have laid down my own desire to be like God and have entered back into your being, reclaimed your image and now I live and move out of you and your love." If we are only bringing people to conviction but not to repentance, we are only bringing them into the woods but not showing them the path out on the other side. We will have merely pointed the finger and condemned them rather than giving them a hope of forgiveness. Not only that, we have once again elevated our own "righteous" selves above them. If we are merely seeking to put a notch in our belt for "another one saved" or wanting people to make a confession of faith to make ourselves feel good about our efforts, we are preaching for selfish motives.

Christ did not come to call the healthy, the righteous, pious and prideful but the sick and those who recognized their illness was killing them. As people of faith, we must realize that we are all on a path of healing. Thus, we must welcome the broken into our Trinitarian community, just as Christ accepts all of us (Romans 15:7).

The difficulty is that acceptance requires immense humility, which naturally fights against the sinful nature. If the nature I am born into says, "Prioritize yourself," this community will be appealing to me only if I don't have to give out love, forgiveness, and mercy to others. My natural predisposition wants what you have to offer, but only if I don't have to offer it myself.

And so goes the church.

And so goes community.

I get the reward with none of the cost. I feel great about myself and bleed the community of its grace and love but never give it back. I withdraw but I don't deposit. I take but I don't give.

And so instead of challenging our communities to bend hearts outward, we have merely accepted a lower standard for what it means to be Christian.

But is it Christ's standard?

We have constructed buildings and developed programs to give people the impression of community and salvation but have merely provided them circles when what they need are squares. We are deceiving people into believing that they can make God just a part of their lives. That they can be a different person inside the church doors than they are outside and that this is okay. That their "spiritual life" is separate than their secular—that the two don't interconnect, that one does not form the other. And although they claim to know God, by their actions they deny him (Titus 1:16) and have therefore accepted God's grace in vain (I Corinthians 15:2; II Corinthians 6:1).

This is not a new phenomenon. Nearly every prophet of the Old Testament spoke to this. Jeremiah says,

> Hear the word of the Lord, all you people of Judah who come through these gates to worship the Lord. This is what the Lord Almighty, the God of Israel, says: Reform your ways and your actions, and I will let you live in this place. Do not trust in deceptive words and say, "This is the temple of the Lord, the temple of the Lord, the temple of the Lord!" If you really change your ways and your actions and deal with each other justly, if you do not oppress the alien, the fatherless or the widow and do not shed innocent blood in

this place, and if you do not follow other gods to your own harm, then I will let you live in this place, in the land I gave your forefathers forever and ever. But look, you are trusting in deceptive words that are worthless.

'Will you steal and murder, commit adultery and perjury, burn incense to Baal and follow other gods you have not known, and then come and stand before me in this house, which bears my Name, and say, "We are safe"—safe to do all these detestable things? Has this house, which bears my Name, become a den of robbers to you? But I have been watching, declares the Lord (Jeremiah 7:2-11).

This is only one example of the many. Jesus essentially says the same thing, as we have already read, during his Sermon on the Mount:

Not everyone who says to me, 'Lord, Lord,' will enter the kingdom of heaven, but only he who does the will of my Father who is in heaven. Many will say to me on that day, "Lord, Lord, did we not prophesy in your name, and in your name drive out demons and perform many miracles?" Then I will tell them plainly, "I never knew you. Away from me, you evildoers" (Matthew 7:21-23)!

The point is that we can't just be "spiritual" on Sundays or when in a church building. Our "spiritual" lives cannot be divorced from who we are. The idea of a "spiritual life" is a new development in Christian thought. This is evident in the fact that the Jews didn't even have a word for "spiritual." They simply assumed that everything you do is spiritual. How you move your hands, your mouth, your eyes and your mind all form your "spiritual life." Because your spirituality is intimately attached to your physicality, what you do with your physical body invades the spiritual realm. Raising your hands in worship then is not only an act of worship but also an act of Spiritual warfare. When you bow your knees in prayer, the act of submission and humility are not only physical but represent more greatly the attitude of your Spirit.

Whatever our bodies do affects our souls. They form our Spirit.

Compartmentalized and fragmented lives are killing Christianity.

God wants our hearts! All of who we are.

But if our hearts are still bent toward our self, they at the same time cannot be aligned with God.

We wear masks that may look like Jesus on the outside but are really just a cheap fabrication. We are not his image, only rarely his resemblance. We must take off our mask and teach others to do the same. The difficulty comes when we see the world through two, one-inch-slits in a cheap mask, it is nearly impossible to see what our own mask looks like. How can we point out someone else's sin when we are blinded to our own? Wouldn't it be far better to remove that which is blinding us, and redirect our own hearts through repentance before we start telling others to do the same? Taking the plank out of our own eye first requires acknowledging it is there. Only then will you "see clearly to remove the speck from the other person's eye" (Matthew 7:5).

The reality is that pointing out someone else's speck in love, even after acknowledging your own plank, greatly offends the sinful nature. As has already been stated, we are not accustomed to this and therefore it only ends in growth and the surgical removal of the speck if the person is aligned with God in love and humility. This assumes that rebuke is done primarily within covenant based community. Condemning the world only leads them further from the love of God. "What business is it of mine to judge those outside the church? Are you not to judge those inside? God will judge those outside" (1 Corinthians 5:12-13). The person who has their sinful nature intact will rarely accept the guidance of another person's correction. Often, instead of humbling themselves to the correction, their first inclination is to form defense mechanisms to protect themselves from the attack.

In *The Screwtape Letters*, C.S. Lewis writes, "The first job of [humans'] Tempters was to harden these choices of the Hell-ward roads into a habit by steady repetition. But then (and this was all-important) to turn the habit into a principle—a principle the creature is prepared to defend."[xxii]

You are not merely attacking one area of their lives. To them, you are attacking who they are. You are attacking something far more personal to the fiber of their being. And when you attack the sinful nature, you are also attacking the devil. And he hates it.

He will fight back.

When our habits have turned into a principle not founded on agape love, we naturally reject the essence of God's image and therefore our humanity. Each time this is done, the devil gains another foothold and his job becomes increasingly easier because the devil's favorite tool of persuasion is for the victim to persuade and deceive themselves. We begin to do the devil's work for him. There comes a time when we begin to believe that the sinful nature *is* our nature; that prioritizing the self is the way humans are supposed to function.

Because of this, we begin to see the world as we wish to see it and become blind to the very problem. The circles have filled the square hole so much as to give us the feeling of fulfillment and purpose but only in the way that a lamp provides light to a room with the blinds open on a summer sunny day. When our hearts become hardened to guidance toward correction, we either avoid or appease the issue, or we become offended, walk away from faith, and in turn, judge those who would dare put on airs of righteousness.

But when you have learned to hide behind a mask your whole life, it no longer becomes a mask but your actual face. It has taken root and very few things can help you to remove it.

Please know, however, you are not without hope, although hope is not easy and it might be painful. Though I suppose no more painful than death will be and therefore the cost is worth every experience it will put you through.

As for your part, if you love someone, you will speak into their life and bring them back to the truth for "whoever turns a sinner from the way of error will save them from death and cover over a multitude of sins" (James 5:20). Speaking into those within your covenant community still wearing masks is a necessary task for life and love to be established because their sin will become yours.

As will their judgment.

If you honestly warn someone of their ways and they fail to listen, you have done what is required of you. You can live your life free of their guilt. There is little left you can do. We shouldn't consume our lives with throwing pearls before swine (Matthew 7:6). There is more kingdom work to be done. Dusting off our cloak and moving on might be the only option left for us (Luke 9:5).

If they persist in their sin: if they don't want to change, if you have warned them once, and then a second time, have nothing to do with them and have them leave your community (1 Corinthians 5:13; Titus 3:10).

Hand them over to Satan (I Corinthians 5:5).

Yea, that sounds harsh.

This is not giving up on the man or woman or secretly hoping for their demise but one last effort in hopes that they may repent, realize who they are, forsake their wicked ways and come back to genuine Trinitarian community. Outside of reciprocating love, we are not fully human; we have no meaning or purpose. When this is finally realized, it could begin the "destruction of their sinful nature so that [their] spirit may be saved on the day of the Lord" (I Corinthians 5:5). This is one final attempt at bringing them to life.

If they are hardened and do not heed your warning, there is little left you can do. They are digging their own graves and they are seemingly eager to finish. They have no desire to change. Hope is something they are cynical to. But if they want life and the great love of God, they will come back—crawling and on their knees, not because they are graveling but because they are humble. Humility and repentance are their only options but both are options that lead to life, away from the devil and towards the face of God.

The Trinitarian God, made known through your community, will have welcomed them, saved them.

Love will have saved them.

Life and Love and Why

chapterfourteen.humanityredeemed
(salvation)

Love will have saved them.

Andy couldn't sleep.

Like many nights before this, his little brother was crying in his bedroom which was next door to Andy's. Andy tried to be empathetic, compassionate even, for he knew that if he had to endure what his brother did, he would be crying too.

John, Andy's brother, was slowing dying from a cancer that was growing in his stomach. The numerous trips to Minnesota to see a specialist and to receive treatment proved to make him feel better but the doctors were convinced that the treatment would not stop his progression toward death, only slow it down.

John was going to die.

Andy did what he could to help John feel better. Many nights, those like this one, Andy would often find his way into his brother's room and sleep alongside him—console him. One summer, Andy saved up all his money so he could take John to the circus, something Andy had wanted to do for him ever since John saw a commercial for it one night on television and couldn't stop talking about it. The experience of the circus left such a lasting impact on John that he decided to make it the theme of his bedroom. Andy wanted to do whatever he could to relieve the pain—if only for a day, a night or an hour.

This night, however, Andy couldn't get out of bed to console his brother. Every breath John took brought him one more closer to death and therefore Andy began to think about this own breathing, his own life; his own death.

But as Andy closed his eyes to picture his own existence after his final day, all he could see was blackness. There was nothing. This imagery feared Andy more than all the pictures of hell he had seen or imagined.

Nothingness; void; blackness.

Alone.

Forever.

As John's crying finally died down as his medicine began to take effect and the pain diminish, Andy was able to fall asleep. But as he passed from being awake to being asleep, one final thought passed through his mind:

Is this really all there is to life? Is that really my destiny?

As a young Christian reading the Bible on my own, I was always under the impression the salvation came with belief. I read passages like Acts 16:31 which says, "Believe in the Lord Jesus Christ and you will be saved—you and your household." I interpreted this command through my own understanding of belief and applied salvation to myself. Although my sinful nature remained intact, I had a cognitive assertion that by believing that Christ physically came, ministered for three years, was killed on the cross and raised again on the third day by God, I would be saved. I "believed in him."

I didn't understand that "belief" in Judaic thought encompassed the entirety of a person. Belief to them meant "trust with your whole heart." Considering that the heart, in their understanding, was the central core of a person, belief meant directing your whole life toward Jesus Christ. Salvation did not come when I received all the information about Jesus and my mind reached the conclusion that he was real and actually did what the Bible says he did.

Salvation rather came when my life was redirected toward God and toward others in agape love, thereby turning from the sin that marked my life (Mark 1:15; Acts 2:38).
Salvation came with repentance, not of a single action, but of my whole sinful nature. And if I am honest, I didn't really repent until late into my college career and only after I was a leader in my youth group, a worship leader of thousands of people city wide, a Bible study leader for high school and college students, and a Biblical and Theological Studies major.

I did all these wonderful Christian things but I did them out of my own power. It was not God who gave me the power to lead the Bible studies or the worship services but my own selfish ambition and desire to be acknowledged for what I was accomplishing for the Kingdom. My actions were like filthy rags before God (Isaiah 54:6) because though they were done in the "name of Christ," they were done for my glory, not God's (John 15:8). I used Christianity as a means to promote myself, my knowledge and how great of a person I was.

My heart was still bent in on itself.

My throne was still established.

And let's be honest, what had I done that needed saving from? I grew up in a middle class home where salvation wasn't a part of my vernacular because I never experienced a situation where I was in need of saving. I was born with a silver spoon in my mouth: a never-ending flow of food, attention, clothing, money, shelter and all other things that made up the "good life." Jesus was an add-on, a ritual we participated in before meals and on Sunday mornings.

Sadly, most of us in western Christendom have been indoctrinated in the faith just like me. For the most part, we have inherited our faith from our parents. I was a Christian because the Christian church was the most accessible venue of worship in my community and because my parents sometimes went. The need of the gospel or of a savior wasn't a reality I experienced, because in our culture, that need is only known by the privileged few. Those who have nothing to hold on to in this world are the ones with the clearest vision of the Kingdom of God (Luke 6:20-22). The rest of us live largely within an apathetic faith because we haven't experienced real need.

Why anticipate or long for good news when we are handed good news everyday by living in the wealthiest nation in the world? Why search for a savior when we don't believe we need salvation? Why should we, when every day we wake up in our comfortable bed, eat from our refrigerator full of food, drive our cars that are full of gas to our work that pays us thousands of dollars a month so that we can buy clothes, food and hours of entertainment for ourselves and our families?

We want for nothing.

When I was younger and looked at the list of behaviors I wasn't supposed to do and noticed that I didn't do any of them, I felt assured of my salvation. I didn't need a savior; I was already doing what was required of me. Compared to the people around me, I was the model Christian. And if they were saved, I was definitely saved.

But notice where this left me: my salvation was assured because I merely believed it existed within a comparative construct. It was on a scale. And because it was comparative, it existed as the way I viewed myself in comparison to the people around me. I was the good Christian and therefore I was saved. But what I failed to realize was that when I said, "I am a good Christian" I was placing myself as the standard for what Christianity was to be about. I put myself on a pedestal and raised myself above all people. And when the pedestal was raised and I was standing on it, I was at the same time lowering all other people before me.

Even my salvation was a matter of self-reign.

I had bought into the belief that Jesus was my "personal savior." Jesus had saved *me* because of all the good things *I* was doing. *I* had a personal relationship with Jesus and it consisted of *me* being great at Christianity: leading *my* Bible studies, *my* youth group, doing *my* devotions, listening to *my* favorite Christian music, wearing *my* "What Would Jesus Do" bracelet and all the while judging and pointing my finger at those who didn't.

The problem for me was that although I had a personal relationship with Jesus, I did not have a communal relationship with Jesus, and because it wasn't communal, it wasn't based on love, which throughout this book we have established as the basis of living the authentic Christian life. My faith was my own, an island unto itself, and my Christian interaction consisted of telling others that they needed to be where I was—that their Christianity lacked that holy spark that mine had.

I know everyone reading this probably hates me right now, or at least who I was. But what I've been describing is a direct and very real implication of having a "personal savior." The very language we use implies that it is all about you and no one else. This, including all the old models of sin already discussed, promotes that your kingdom can be established along side, and even within, God's. But it can't. Because if it's "all about you," it can't at the same time be all about the other. And if it isn't about the other, it can't be about love. And if it isn't about love, it can't be about God's kingdom. And if it's not about God's kingdom, it is about your own.

You can't save yourself. You can save no one. You are only a fool.

As am I.

I live more out of my stupidity, short-sightedness and personal kingdom than I do out of my love. What I need to do—what we all need to do—is allow God to turn our hearts back to him (1 Kings 18:37). And doing this requires that we not only accept Jesus' forgiveness for our foolishness (Ephesians 2:8-9), but also act on that forgiveness by living out of agape love like Christ. If we do not, we have gained no ground in our search for meaning, life, or our humanity. Our grace remains cheap.

Salvation is not a reality we can claim for ourselves.

Dietrich Bonhoeffer says, "Cheap grace means the justification of sin without the justification of the sinner. Grace alone does nothing, they say, and so everything can remain as it was before."[xxiii]

When we abuse grace, we abuse Christ. In our culture, grace and Christ have become the means to an end—our own salvation—not the transforming presence of God to change lives. We are only "godless people, who pervert the grace of our God into a license for immorality and deny Jesus Christ our only Sovereign and Lord" (Jude 4).
Grace without repentance is our condemnation.

To this end, grace is both frightening and dangerous to those who exist out of self-reign, because it demands something of its recipients. At the very least, it demands we accept it for what it is: a gift that is not self-gratifying, but other-oriented.

It is dangerous because the one who gives it is dangerous: "I will show you whom you should fear: fear him who, after the killing of the body, has power to throw you into hell. Yes, I tell you, fear him" (Lk 12:5). But grace is not a danger to the one who accepts it. He or she who ignores and opposes God will have his grace come back to bight them. Do not shun grace. In the end it will either be your glory or your judgment; your life or your death; your heaven or your hell.

We want to receive gifts we can repay, to get ourselves "off the hook," but grace is an undeserved favor. I was once told, "Grace is getting what we don't deserve, whereas mercy is not getting what we do deserve." Grace, at its foundation, is charity. Grace is the expression of God's love for us, and accepting it therefore requires obedience to agape love (John 14:23, 15:10). One cannot accept grace without also accepting the life of love.

God's love, in other words, is synonymous with his grace.

It was *because* of his love that he offered us grace in the first place! Indeed, from the very beginning, our lives have been full of sin, love, and grace: sin through our own self-reign, grace and love from God. When we repent through accepting his grace, we therefore become the vessels by which God's love is manifested in the world. Thus, the person who does not recognize themselves as sinful cannot accept grace.

Grace and sin cannot coexist.

This does not necessitate a Wesleyan doctrine of perfected sanctification (the idea, supported by the 18th century theologian John Wesley, that those who are in Christ are without sin), but merely points out that we are indeed sinners. Grace exists for us when we realize we need it. The prodigal son did not take a step toward home until he realized that in his current state, death was his only option. God's grace will continue our sanctification, but we must first willingly acknowledge our sinfulness. It is only by our shifting disposition—turning around—that we become sanctified, that is, holy before God.

Many believe that they must live a certain way in order to receive grace. This was the story of my life ten years ago. But works do not open the door by which God extends grace; they instead slam the door shut, deadbolt it and throw the furniture against it. Works are our selfish attempt to climb onto the throne of God—but he will not have it. We can only accept what he offers us in humility.

So is it fair to say that God loves us where we are? If we equate love with grace, and believe that grace and sin cannot coexist, is it fair to say love and sin can? The obvious answer is no. Am I then saying that God does not love the sinner? To answer this, we must first understand that a simple "no" is really only half the answer. God's love is always emanating out from him to the sinner, but this does not necessitate that the sinner accepts or even desires God's love.

For most, it is too frightening. It asks too much of them.

Accepting God's love requires that we engage on a journey. Where does the road lead? To God himself. If it ends in any other destination, the journey will have been for not.

Pointless.

What is most beautiful about this road is that it gets narrower the longer you travel on it. In the beginning, the road may be as wide as the world and encompass all the world offers you. The longer you travel on the road of love that leads only to God, however, you will notice how the world seems to slip off the edge and becomes irrelevant. In the end, all that is left is the love of God which leads you further into the love of others.

But remember, love requires progress through action.

The prodigal son did not experience reconciliation and redemption until he made the journey home. He had to turn from his old life, turn to face the father and begin to move in a new direction (Luke 15:20). He would have done a great thing if he would have only turned around but for salvation to be made true requires sanctification—it requires that once you have turned around, that you move in a new direction.

Thus, stagnancy in faith gives us the impression of salvation but only in the way an opposing king surrenders but doesn't leave his throne. Surrender is only in his head, not his heart. True salvation is one that is actively working to keep the face of God in sight.

Please know however that there is no minimum speed of which you must travel on the road toward God. Some travel much faster than others. Some are provided easier lots in life. Some are born into very loving families that instill within their children the call to love. Some are not. As long as you are on this road, albeit narrow and because of the nature of our world, hard to find, you are in a good place. The longer you are on it, the more your pace will quicken.

But also know that adults cannot live off of food intended for babies. Those who ought to be spiritual adults and running at a dead sprint but are still finding their sustenance in spiritual milk, crawling, might consider revising the way the view themselves (Hebrews 5:13). Milk is for babies.

"But solid food is for the mature, who by constant use have trained themselves to distinguish good from evil" (Hebrews 5:14).

Love from hate.

Therefore, when the Trinitarian God bound in reciprocating love defines us, instead of our reign, salvation should be a present reality. Love defeats sin and provides life. God's heart and essence has once again become ours—his image is reclaimed. If our salvation rests in God's grace through our faith in Christ (Ephesians 2:8), we must understand that faith then is not merely the capacity for belief, but a binding of oneself to Christ's life, suffering and resurrection (Romans 8:17).

Because Christ came to save all humanity, anyone who looks into the face of God to share in this disposition has salvation. A "personal savior," then, doesn't make sense because Christ is not only mine—he is ours. As Christ relates the forgiveness and agape of God to us, so we who profess to follow him are to extend that forgiveness and agape to those who still need it. The person whose defining disposition is agape love rooted in Christ shares Christ's salvation. In this way, salvation is communal because it exists for a certain type of person.

It is corporate.

There are only two types of people: those who occupy God's kingdom; and those who occupy their own.

Those whose hearts are bent outward toward God; and those whose hearts are bent inward upon themselves.

Those who love; and those who hate.

Those who bear good fruit; and those who produce bad fruit (Matthew 7:16-19).

Those who are on the narrow road which leads to God; and those who are on the wide road which leads to destruction (Matthew 7:13-14).

Jacobs; and Esaus (Romans 9:13).

One is saved. One is not.

Furthermore, salvation is communal because it demands you serve others in love holistically. It requires the entirety of who you are be devoted to making known God's love through service. Because of this, only those who have reoriented themselves to the presence of God—turned around—receive the salvation of Christ. We cannot serve others if our hearts are still bent inwards on ourselves.

Paul emphasized that we are to do nothing out of "selfish ambition...but in humility consider others better than ourselves" (Philippians 2:3). Because our "attitude should be the same as that of Christ Jesus; who, being in very nature God, did not consider equality with God something to be grasped, but made himself nothing...he humbled himself" (Philippians 2:3, 6-8). The parallel is clear: we humans who have tried to take on the nature of God and make ourselves his equal ought to remember that the true God, Jesus Christ, humbled himself to die in order to save his people. He was then lifted to the seat of highest honor (Philippians 2:9). To be a ruler is not to have all the power—that is the devil's lie we unfortunately believed—but to live out of agape love. Thus, these verses form the basis of what salvation means. We must be bound in agape love. To do this, Paul follows by encouraging us to "continue to work out our salvation" (Philippians 2:12) by being obedient in the same way Christ was: through humility. Only when we are bound in sacrificial love—agape love—will we too share in his resurrection and be lifted with him to the place of highest honor.

The irony of it all is that we achieve only in Christ what we sought in the self: deification. We enter into the divine life through grace only when we give up our own search for it. When our search is for Christ and not our own glorification, we will achieve the only thing we ever wanted: to be like God—but in fact we achieve infinitely more, we will be *in* Christ.

This means that we take up your cross and follow Christ (Matthew 16:24). That is, die to yourself, your reign, your priority and your will. But it must be killed—all of it. It cannot simply be defeated but allowed to remain living. If sin reigns over any part of you, it reigns over all of you.

As George MacDonald said, "There is no heaven with a little of hell in it."[xxiv] There is no life with a little of death in it. There is no love with a little of hate in it. There are only two roads. You cannot travel on both for they move in opposite directions.

When God defines us, all of our interactions will be undergirded by the love of God empowering us to love one another. Our mind will be the mind of Christ; our heart, his heart: our will, his will.

Salvation is cooperation with God's Spirit. It is reentering the Trinitarian God. There is synergy involved. After all, salvation is Christ's; we only receive it by participating in him (Psalm 13:5; 27:1; Romans 5:2, 9-11).

But this all gives us just a little too much credit in the process. Although our interactions of love will be innumerable, they will not be enough to buy our salvation or our sanctification. Because, truthfully, it's not about doing but only about being and it is God's Spirit that provides us our new-found being. We will fail in our doing every single day. Sometimes we may fail in ways that we never thought imaginable. Sometimes we may fail in ways by doing things that only "terrible people" do.

But thank God that his grace is sufficient to cover our sin (2 Corinthians 12:9).

Thank God that repentance is available.

But we ask, "How could anyone possibly live every interaction out of love? I sin so much in this life. How could it ever be the case that my life is defined by love and God through every interaction??

But the very question still assumes salvation is about me and what I can do.

So how can anyone be saved?

"With human beings, this is impossible, but with God all things are possible" (Matthew 19:26).

What differentiates me as being bound to Christ from the rest of the world and its religions is that I acknowledge I cannot be saved by my own efforts. By my own efforts, I cannot do good (Romans 3:10-23). I therefore appeal to God's grace and great love and in faith, respond to them in a like manner.

Jesus nowhere said that dying to ourselves would be easy, that crucifying our reign would be painless. Shedding our predisposition (shifting our orientation from self-lovers to other lovers) is a very difficult task in part because *we* cannot do it.
But for those who are willing, God can in them.

Salvation, then, is more about accepting God's Spirit than it is working to achieve it. It is the realization of our own inability manifested in humility and love as we respond to God's great love on our behalf.

Jesus has promised us that we are not in it alone. What seems impossible is not when you have the omnipotent God on your side (Matthew 19:26). As long as we continue to die daily to our reign, acknowledge when we fail, willingly allow God to pick us up and turn ourselves around, we will see the face of God.

He will embrace us with open arms.

chapterfifteen.redeeminghumanity
(call)

He will embrace us with open arms.

Life and Love and Why

The tears fell from Leila's eyes and splashed against the picture of her daughter, Hannah, she held in her hand. She wanted so badly to be a different person than her father. She thought of her father being put to death, and she was tempted to turn her television on again to see what the reporters were saying about him. "How does the world interpret someone like her father? Wicked? Hate-filled? Depraved? Is there any good left inside of him?" Her mind was racing as she reached for the remote.

But she stopped. Her fear of her father and how he reminded her of herself left her unable to move.

"But does anyone really deserve that? Is anyone really good?" She looked again at the picture of Hannah. "Why am I not on death row awaiting my punishment? How is what I have done really any different?" Leila had known that abandoning her daughter was a mistake but by the time she realized it, she was sure Hannah hated her and there was no way she could show her face to see the pain and hurt she was sure Hannah's face would reveal. She had convinced herself that even if she wanted to find her, to say she was sorry, that she wouldn't even know where to start.

And so she never did.

As Leila sat at her kitchen table the next day, the heading on the newspaper hit her like a brick. "30 year old case finally finds justice." She tried hard to mourn for her father but realized that she was only mourning his reflection in her.

"How is this the life I have chosen?!" Leila slammed her hand against the table in anger and in the process spilt her coffee all over the newspaper sprawled out on her table. She ran to the sink to grab a towel and as she padded down the paper, a different heading caught her eye.

"Girl looking to give up 'Hope.'" Leila was intrigued for she was thinking the same thing about herself. She continued. "Hannah Moore may be young," the article read, "but she is far wiser than the increasingly rising number of pregnant teens who are deciding to keep their babies, even though many admit they cannot afford to raise them in healthy environments."

"The article is decidedly biased," Leila thought as she pondered if this Hannah could be her Hannah.

"Hannah, the sixteen year old mother of Hope, said 'I never had a mom. I have no idea how to raise a child. I desire for my daughter to have a better life than I had. I hope she will make better choices in life and someone other than me can better help her to do that.'

Leila intently read through the article, and when she reached the bottom, tears fell once again, adding to the already soaking wet page in front of her. She knew this Hannah Moore was hers. "Hope is currently in foster care. If you are interested in adopting one of the roughly 550,000 children currently living in foster care, please contact your loc..."

The tears filling Leila's eyes left her unable to see and therefore read.

All the information Leila needed was in front of her. Hannah was approachable and findable. Leila's heart was pounding as she thought of the possibilities in front of her. She understood that in front of her were only two roads. One lead her deeper and deeper in to despair, frustration, pity and apathy and the other toward healing the biggest wound she had ever made.

"Hannah is only three hours away," Leila was talking to herself, something she did when she was in deep contemplation. "I can't not go to her. If she hates me and wants nothing to do with me, at least I have done my part. All I can do is try, right? Oh, Leila..." The pounding of her heart was deafening to her inner voice. The choice was before her. One step in one of two directions could either free her or continue to imprison her. "But I'm scared. All I can do is try. I have to try, if nothing else, for Hope's sake. They need to know I love them. I have to find Hannah.

I have to find Hope."

I was once asked, "What does salvation look like when it is given hands and feet?"

I think the answer is simple: it looks like Jesus. When salvation is given a body, it is a body directed toward agape love for others. But notice what this requires of us:

When our hands take up love, they move only to serve others.

When our feet take up love, they travel only to extend the love of Jesus to others.

When our eyes take up love, they see only to identify the needs of others.

When our ears take up love, they listen for the cries of the oppressed, and hear rebuke when we are wrong.

When our tongues take up love, they speak only to encourage, to rebuke and to instill hope, grace, forgiveness, mercy and worth in those around us.

When our bodies take up love, they become the temple of the living God, members of Christ himself, one with him in Spirit (I Corinthians 6:15, 17, 19).

But love is a deep and mysterious well that will be explored for the rest of your life, and no matter how deep you go, you will find that even then you will have only rippled the surface. I will never know what love looks like in every situation, thought, action or word spoken. I know love is absolute and exists whenever I actively give of myself so that others will receive life, but I often have difficulty determining what that looks like. I don't know what Jesus would do in my particular situation. All I have is his example and a call. All I know is that I am called to prioritize you before myself.

And it really doesn't matter who you are. It is still my calling.

The problem is that we only see the world through our finite perspective, so we will never know the far-reaching consequences of our present actions. The best we can do on this side of eternity is give of ourselves whenever we are able to.

But we are only fools: we don't really know anything. We must therefore rely on God's grace and forgiveness to lift us up when we fail. And we will fail. Every day we will fail. Remember, there is only one sin that is ever committed: the prioritizing of yourself as you exert your reign and power. The potential for sin exists then with every thought, action and word that you have.

It is thought that the average person has roughly 3000 intentional thoughts per day[xxv]—and everyone of these shape you.

It is also thought that the average person makes roughly 5000 active, conscious decisions every day[xxvi]—and every one of these shape you.

In addition to that, the average person speaks nearly 440 sentences per day (nearly 7000 words)[xxvii]—and every one of these shape you.

So, on any given day, there are approximately 8440 experiences you have where sin might reign. If there is this much potential for sin however, there is equal potential for love for one is the antithesis of the other.

The heart bent toward God is the heart that will grow in the understanding of their failure in order that they will grow in the understanding of their love, Jesus and Trinitarian living. If we love whenever we are able, grow in the knowledge of love, and take into account our life experiences, our ability and capacity to love will increase. I believe this is what we call "wisdom."

But growing in wisdom involves the entirety of your being. As we showed above, you are being formed through every activity you participate in. Your decisions determine your destiny: Everything you do—what you eat or drink, what you do with your hands, your feet, your eyes, ears, and tongue—will bring you in the end to one of two conclusions: eternal life or eternal death.

Shouldn't we as Christians then be more eager to live our lives in such a way that will form us in the end as those who have chosen life? Shouldn't we live more earnestly in love in all we do and passionately explore what love is in every circumstance?

If you've made that decision for life in God, you will quickly discover what I mean about love being a very deep mystery. You will question every decision you make and whether these decisions exhibit love. You will want to know what love looks like at any given time for if no other reason than in love and God is the source of life and joy. Most importantly, though, you will quickly notice that the sacrifices love asks of you will drastically change the way you live your life in our culture and in our world.

This is precisely why so few choose to engage in it—or that they choose to engage in it only when it is convenient for them. This is unfortunately why the narrow road is not wider than it is. (Matthew 7:13-14) And this is unfortunately why only a remnant will be saved (Romans 11:5). And this is unfortunately why God only reserved 7000 in all of Israel that would not bow down to worthless idols promoted by their culture (I Kings 19:18).

Love requires much of those who engage in it.

So, unfortunately, many don't.

Because God is the counter-cultural force, love is the counter-cultural force.

If culture is defined as the behaviors and belief characteristics of a particular group of people, it is by its definition relative and subjective. It moves with the waves of ideas, shaped and molded by the given characteristics, beliefs and mentalities of those that make up a particular culture. In other words, culture is worldly. If it is worldly, it is laced with self-reign. But love is absolute, steadfast and enduring. It, like God, does not change like shifting shadows but maintains its purpose in every and all situations. As culture is worldly, love is counter-cultural because it is other worldly.

Consider this: our Western culture tells us that we should look a certain way and do what is necessary to achieve that look. We therefore spend, as a nation, over 55 billion dollars annually on dietary supplements, gym memberships and fitness equipment and 82 billion dollars annually on new clothing to make ourselves look like the models in magazines.

Paradoxically, however, our culture tells us that fast food is good food. Most fast food meals are notorious for being high in sodium, trans-fat and partially hydrogenated oils. Translation: they are terrible for your body. Yet, we spend 134 billion dollars a year on all the various fast food chains which has surged our nation to where 63% of us are overweight and 31% are obese.

Our culture tells us that celebrities are more important than you or I. We therefore, on average, watch 2 hours and 50 minutes of television daily. This is nine times the amount of time we spend on all other leisurely activities combined.

Our culture tells us that we ought to have the best of everything, but for the cheapest price: to get the most out of our money. Our culture also tells us that credit cards are the most appropriate means to get what we want in life. The average American household therefore has over 8000 dollars in credit card debt alone. What our culture doesn't tell us is that some of our stores pay their employees unfairly so that the savings can be given to you, the consumer. Our culture also doesn't inform us that many of the products for sale are produced in a sweatshop by a child who was denied an education and normal childhood, working 80 hour weeks at 30 cents an hour.

This need to spend infiltrates our holidays as well. Our culture tells us that Easter needs to be celebrated with candy to make it more appealing. We therefore spend over 1.5 billion dollars a year on Easter candy alone. And Christmas is more disturbing. Our culture demands that Christmas be celebrated with gifts. We therefore spend nearly 500 billion dollars on Christmas presents annually.

Our culture tells us that our worth comes from what we have. One in 11 American families invest in self-storage units occupying 1.875 billion square feet of space. The self-storage industry revenue has exceeded that of Hollywood. Besides this, we spend nearly 80 percent of our free time taking care of the things we purchase.

Finally, our culture tells us that if you are not spending money, you are hurting the economy; that you are un-American. We are therefore given "stimulus" checks to help boost our spending. The assumption is that if we had more money, we would spend it on ourselves.

But is the culture the guide by which we should direct our lives? Should we just "go with the flow?" Should we just "do what the Romans do" and "conform to the pattern of this world" (Romans 12:2)? Do we even know what we are doing when abiding by and following the culture's mores?

Have we ever seriously asked ourselves the above questions?

God bless America?

I think he already has.

While the average per capita income in a U.S. household is over 46,000 dollars, the average per capita income for the entire world is just under 8000 U.S. dollars. What is even more astonishing is that the average per capita income in the least developed nation is 491 U.S. dollars. These are often the people that do not have medicine to fight off curable diseases, such as malaria, which they contracted because they can't afford a ten dollar net to cover their beds. Not only do these people have almost no opportunities for education, about half of them will die before they reach the twelfth grade. Only about half these countries' populations have clean drinking water (not to mention proper sanitation) and only ever *dream* of taking a bath or shower.

And these are the people who are making *our* clothes; our toys; our luxuries.

Today, we exist as a global society. One hundred years ago, the average person couldn't tell you what was happening in Africa or Honduras. They didn't know. To "love your neighbor" literally meant to "love the people in the house next to you." However, in the current day, our neighbor may not live next door but next-continent. By the extensive reach of global media and the Internet, the world is far more accessible. I can now see how my 46,000 dollar salary could meet a host of the basic needs of impoverished families in Africa or Asia. Our culture does not limit our ability to love; it simply does not make it a priority. The heart of our culture is bent in on itself.

So here we are, 46000 dollars wealthier buying Easter candy, Christmas presents, gym memberships, dietary supplements, new cars, new clothing, new homes, new televisions to idolize celebrities, storage units to store all our stuff that we bought with all our money, food from fast food chains that slowly kill us, and when we have purchased more than our income will allow, we simply transition our buying to credit cards.

Is this loving?

Because if it's not, don't do it. You will only be serving the Devil.

Every day we are faced with thousands of decisions. Will we shop at those stores that purchase their products from sweatshops even though it might save me a dollar or two? Or will we say "no", spend a little more of our money and not contribute to the system of slavery that exists in our world? Will we purchase "greener" vehicles that might not get as many miles to the gallon, might cost a little more money up-front but that don't produce as many carbon emissions that are slowly killing our planet? Will we buy our produce from local farmers so that a truck does not have to drive hundreds of miles from a corporate farm that is being subsidized by the government to produce more vegetables to make ethanol from but at the same time are laced with toxic amounts of chemical fertilizer that will run through our rivers, into our oceans and kill thousands of square miles of aquatic life? Will we hold on to bottles, paper and other recyclable goods until we find a proper recycling disposal for them or will we just throw them away because it's easier for me even though they will sit for a thousand years in a land-fill? Will we wait in line for a 7 dollar cup of coffee and neglect to extend mercy and grace to the person in need on the street corner behind us? Will we even begin to be aware of where our products are being made, where our coffee comes from, what we are spending our money on and simply the people around us on the local and global scene? Will we spend hundreds if not thousands of dollars at casinos when there are twenty-five thousand children who die daily from hunger related issues? Will we gossip and slander our brothers and sisters simply because "the tabloids and media do it?" Will we wear risqué clothing because it is the norm of our culture even though it is making our brothers and sisters stumble and at the same time objectifying ourselves? Will we occupy our time with television and sporting events and at the end of the day say we have no time to pray, be in God's word or serve our community? Will we buy into who our culture and the world tell us we need to be? Are we just living "on earth in luxury and self-indulgence:" fattening ourselves for the day of slaughter (James 5:5)? Are we just befriending the world and "playing" Christian? Do we not know that friendship with the world means hatred of God (James 4:4)?

Love is indeed a deep and mysterious well.

Because in some way, shape or form, all of those questions are questions of love.

If love of the world means hatred of God, then love of God must mean hatred of the world. We know the things of the world do not offer life because their source is temporal (i.e. finite humans). So why do we play around with them? When the seed of the world is planted in someone, what grows inside of them feels very much like power, control, fulfillment and success. It feels good but only in the way that scratching an itch feels good.

There is a deeper cut that needs to be healed.

In his book, *The Screwtape Letters,* C.S. Lewis writes, "Prosperity knits a man to the world. He feels that he is 'finding his place in it,' while really it is finding its place in him."[xxviii] It is not that we are finding fulfillment, purpose and success in the world but rather that Satan—the "prince of this world" (John 12:30; Ephesians 2:2)—is finding success in us. It only feels right because it greatly appeals to our manipulated nature.

But it is not true.

Nor is it real.

It is only a shadow of a deeper and more authentic life. We are rather called to give of ourselves in the same way God gave of himself (John 15:12). In this pursuit alone is the life that will be meaningful and purposeful. Whether it is by the world's standards is no business of ours.

And quite frankly, we shouldn't care.

If you were on the titanic and you knew it was going down, wouldn't you take the opportunity to get off of it? Or would you rather stay at the bar, sip your martini and enjoy the music?

Life is found in agape love because God is love.

We are called to take up our cross and die to our selfish ambition, reign and priority. We are called to enter into true fellowship, the type of community that says, "If I have, I will give; if you are in need, please receive." We are called to re-enter the triune God.

When Abraham received the promise that he would "be blessed," the blessings he received were only offered to him in order that he might bless others (Genesis 12:2). We are called to do the same. The definition of "blessing" is not simply "a gift" but "a gift that moves you into action." We have been given what we have so that we might bless others: we are blessed to be a blessing. As Jesus says, "For everyone who has been given much, much will be demanded; and from the one who has been entrusted with much, much more will be asked" (Luke 12:48).

As a culture, we are blessed. But the blessings of wealth and material possessions are on the shallow end of God's good gifts, not because the gifts aren't good but because they are easier to give away. By their nature, those things that are outside of yourself require less sacrifice on your part to get rid of. And while philanthropy is great, it is not the kingdom of God. Your time and energy, sweat, blood, and tears, prayers and general presence are far greater gifts because they require infinitely more of who you are.

They require all of you.

Humanity, at the deepest fabric of its being does not long after stuff—it longs for community. We crave intimacy, that connection with someone who genuinely cares for us as a unique individual. The person who deeply longs for stuff is becoming less human with every new item bought. Nothing of this world is eternal except the soul, the breath of God. So what good is it if we gain the whole world and all its possessions but in the mean time forfeit our soul (Matthew 16:26)?

The greater gifts are those we take for granted: eyes to see God's beautiful creation; ears to hear laughter and beautiful music; legs to walk, skip, and play with our children; lungs that allow us to breathe, talk and sing; God's image in our souls; Jesus' sacrifice on our behalf; the love of God; God himself...

Because the greater gifts are simple, they are often forgotten. Besides that, because these gifts are placed within a sinful world, they are sometimes twisted, unevenly distributed and perhaps even painful. It is like giving a pack of wolves a slab of meat. It is a good gift, but not all will get the chance to eat the best parts.

Every breath we take and each day we have is a precious gift. God is not required to extend grace, mercy, love and forgiveness to sinful humanity, and yet he does by sustaining our lives. And because this is the case, we are called to extend these great gifts to others.

Our lives are not our own. We were bought at a price (I Corinthians 7:23). We too ought to give of ourselves to the point of death. However, for many this will not be martyrdom, but rather living in radical and generous agape until the day you die.

With every thought you think, be in constant prayer. With every sight you see, acknowledge God as a wonderful creator. With every word you speak, preach love and truth. With every bite of food taken, be grateful and remember those who this day will go hungry. With every breath you take, remember whose air you breathe and be thankful. With every beat of your heart, remember whose blood was shed for you. With every movement of your hands, serve someone. With every step you take, bring the great news of Jesus Christ, his love and how he saved you.

Let love not be something that is done only when it is comfortable or convenient. That would be a great offense to the God who does not change, hinder or stumble in his extension of blessing, grace and love. God desires that we give as much grace and love as we have received. Considering that God's grace and love are what sustains us at any given moment, our call then is to extend grace and love at all moments.

This is precisely why the Spirit of God living through us is at war against the world. It is a fight. Everyday a battle is being waged against the world, its power, its prince and its wisdom. It promotes you as the one and only priority. What's worse is that it makes sense. Directed away from God, our only priority is our self. We are the only one that really matters. It seems really wise to take matters into your own hands, become angry and upset when you are offended, don't you deserve better? Do you want what someone else has? Take it, or at least complain that you can't have it. Don't be content with your life. You deserve better. It's all about you, after all. Do what makes you feel good and happy.

It would be foolish of you to give of your hard earned money so that someone who is without shelter might not sleep on a sidewalk but in a bed for a night. It would be foolish of you to interact with, include and care for a co-worker who you know feels left out, neglected and unappreciated. That takes energy and actually getting to know someone. It would be foolish of you to walk or bike to work so you don't contribute to green house gasses and to reduce your carbon footprint. It would be foolish of you to save your money rather than buy yet another blue shirt when you already have five in your closet. It would be foolish of you to take the saved money and feed a starving child with it. It would be foolish of you to spend your time in prayer over issues around our world. It would be foolish of you to be thankful, say please and be hospitable to others. It would be foolish of you to speak up against gossip and slander when you hear it amongst your friends. It would be foolish of you to consider another person's humanity when looking at their body on your computer or in a magazine. It would be foolish of you to control your tongue when you are frustrated.

All these require sacrifice. Who wants that?

It's foolish because the wisdom of the world says you are what is most important. It is appealing because it promotes you above all other people, but unfortunately at the sake of all other people.

You deserve better in this life.

But thank God he doesn't give you what you deserve.

What you deserve is death.

And yet, here you are.

The wisdom of God, on the other hand, is first of all humble and sacrificial and it is foolish to those who are wise in the ways of the world. If you operate on the assumption that what you have earned gives you license to ignore those around you, you are working out of the wisdom of the world. "Such wisdom does not come down from heaven but is earthly, unspiritual, of the devil. For where you have envy and selfish ambition, there you find disorder and every evil practice" (James 3:15-16).

But God says, "I will destroy the wisdom of the wise; the intelligence of the intelligence I will frustrate" (I Corinthians 1:18).

It seems foolish that an innocent man would willingly be put to death so that someone else might experience life; but this is the wisdom of God.

This is the love of God in its fullest form.

And it is this love manifested in us that can and will transform our world. We are only fools but fools who are willing to take up our cross, share in Christ's death and help bring others into our redemption for the same "Spirit of him who raised Jesus from the dead is living in [us]" (Romans 8:11).

We too can raise the dead.

We too can change the world.

We too can participate in Christ's redemptive act as we see the opportunity to love on all occasions. And even though we will a fight until the day we die and even though there will be days when we feel defeated by our inability to love as we should and even though there will be days when the world is nothing but trouble for us, we should take heart, for Jesus Christ has overcome the world (John 16:33). He has defeated death and Satan and we can share in his victory. Death has been swallowed up in victory (I Corinthians 15:54)!

Our call is to love. It is a simple yet incredibly profound call. It is a task that will take us our entire life to accomplish and it will be accomplished not because we will have fulfilled our ability to do so but because we will have endured (Hebrews 12:1-3). And although we may not know what most of the expressions of love look like, we are called to search and continually explore the well that will prove itself to be deep and mysterious.

The exploration begins now.

So often we walk through our halls, our home, our stores, our offices and malls without even considering that we are surrounded by people who need the love of God.

Recognize the humanity around you.

Let us open our eyes. Let us see with God's eyes the worth in every human person. Let us hear with God's ears those who silently cry for justice. Let us speak with God's words truth to a world founded on lies. Let our hearts beat with the compassion of the Almighty love. Let us use our hands in the humble way of Christ, take up a basin and a towel and serve others rather than be served. And with every step, let us move our feet to God's movement, the movement of love. Let us live out of love. Let us be defined by the Trinitarian God.

It begins with a single decision on your part. And when that decision is made, it will begin again with another.

And another.

And another.

The action of Love, even if perceived to be minor, is always radical because it is born out of a radical God. It is always great. It will always produce fruit. It will always grow. It will always expand. But the Kingdom of God does not expand necessarily by adding more people but in those people's deepening of the quality of their love for one another. The earliest Rabbis understood that in every act of love, the entirety of the Kingdom of God became realized. No act of love is therefore insignificant. But they also understood that in every act of sin, the entirety of Satan's work was realized.

"If serving the Lord seems undesirable to you, then choose for yourselves this day whom you will serve" (Joshua 24:15). Will you serve yourself and thereby Satan? Or will you choose agape love, to serve others and thereby God?

After all, God is love.

Jesus is therefore love.

We are the extension of Jesus' ministry to the world.

We are indwelled with his Spirit (Acts 1:8).

But the life that is indwelled with the Spirit of Christ will have a byproduct. Paul said that the fruit of the Spirit are "Love, joy, peace, patience, kindness, goodness, faithfulness, gentleness and self-control" (Galatians 5:22-23). Is it fair to say that if a life is not exhibiting these characteristics, that the Spirit of Christ is not actually indwelling it?

Because if all we do is put on the "Jesus mask" and pretend Christian, the great love of God will never be realized in our world. Love isn't something we actually care about and therefore neither is God.

But if God is love and his Spirit truly indwells us, then we are love.

We too are the great hope of a broken world.

We wonder why God just doesn't come down in his immense power and fix everything. But we quickly forget Calvary. We quickly forget that Jesus was disfigured beyond that of any human being and his form marred beyond human likeness. We forget that he was despised and rejected by others and that we held him in low esteem. We forget that he took our pain and bore our suffering. We forget that he was pierced for our transgressions and crushed for our iniquities (Isaiah 52:14-53:5).

We forget that God has acted mightily on our behalf. What else could love have done? "After he has suffered, he will see the light of life and be satisfied...for he bore the sin of many, and made intercession for the transgressor" (Isaiah 53:11-12). We are redeemed. Love has saved us. And now he has instilled within us the task to love one another as he has loved us (John 15:12).

We are his redemptive participants.

God never said he would work for us to transform our world. He did say that if we are willing, he would work through us.

Let today be the day we say "Yes, Lord, we are willing."

Life and Love and Why

Appendix

Unfortunately, the idea of a "spiritual discipline" suggests that one particular activity is spiritual where perhaps others are not. I hope you understand that everything you do in life impacts and forms your spirit. There are no specific spiritual disciplines because every step you take is a discipline of the Spirit. My hope in writing this book was that you would come to acknowledge that everything you do ought to be done in love and therefore form your spirit in a certain way: a way that is bent toward and aligned with God.

Nonetheless, below are some brief and simple thoughts regarding some of what have classically been called "spiritual disciplines." A discipline is something that is done to train you to be a certain way. The classical disciplines are confession, submission, baptism, communion, worship, fasting, prayer, service, meditation, study, simplicity, and solitude. You will notice that I only comment on about half of them. Instead, I have decided to comment on ten other Christian "practices" that I believe are relevant to the modern reader: community, marriage, raising children, reconciliation, sabbath, missions, evangelism, giving, baptism, and evangelism.

And what you will quickly notice about these practices is that they ask you to engage holistically, that is, with all of who you are. These things are not just compartmentalized in your Christian box where you keep your Christian characteristics. They require all of you.

Confession

Acknowledging that we are indeed bent toward self-reign is the first step toward correcting it. It takes a strong yet humble person to admit they have been wrong or have wronged someone. Without this crucial realization, repentance cannot take place, because true repentance means turning around from our sinful nature, and thus the sin that accompanies it.

But why can't we simply acknowledge our sin, keep it to ourselves, turn from it and continue to live our life? Why must we confess it? First,

Jesus said that what comes out of your mouth is an overflow of your heart. Putting words to your disgust of your sin is a powerful act in and of itself because it takes it out of your head and begins the process of applying it to your heart.

Second, because sin is also a communal problem, you need to acknowledge your sin within community. Confessing your sin in front of a mirror is a good start at making it real but it does very little in helping you turn from it.

We need one another to assist us in our turning toward God. If you leave your brothers and sisters oblivious to how your sinful nature is manifesting itself in your life, you will be fighting the battle alone.

And there is no such thing as a one-man army.

Not a successful one anyway.

Community

The church was designed to exist as a body of those who have reoriented their life toward reciprocating love for one another as a Trinitarian community. Together it strives to grow in its ability and capacity to love God and others. Jesus' declaration that "on this rock, I will build my church" (Matthew 16:18) was the declaration that the foundation of the church would be Jesus himself—Jesus God's Messiah—who would redeem humanity. The embodiment and personification of love was to be the establishment of the church. Not a building (although they can be helpful) nor a saint.

Genuine community therefore exists when two or more people gather together under the headship of Christ to proclaim his Lordship through their love for one another. When it is done in a reciprocating fashion, no needs go un-met, sin is defeated and redemption is manifested. This was the ethos of the first church community and although we live in a different time and our structures and systems have changed, the ethos should not.

Marriage

Sadly, in our current culture, more marry out of eros than they do out of agape. When the euphoria dies off, we interpret our feelings as "no longer being in love" and we move onto to a different spouse who will provide us with that old sense of sexual tension. We have interpreted lust as love, have married out of our sinful nature. Without the foundation of agape, our marriage becomes more about us than God or our spouse.

Marriage, like community and church, was to be the embodiment and reflection of God himself. God created a spouse for Adam so that he would not have to be alone. Like the Trinity, a man and his wife would become one in reciprocating love. As one of God's greatest gifts, it was designed to be first directed toward God, and only then toward one another. A marriage based on reciprocating love is the only marriage that will continue to be full of joy and have the support to endure a life-time.

Unfortunately, our modern churches have often quarreled over this very simple fact through the debate as to what it means to "submit" to one another (e.g. Ephesis 5:21ff). We should always remember that mutual submission first means mutually submitting to God. Both husband and wife must die to their reign and each take their cross into marriage.

Wives, wouldn't you want to submit to your husband if he continually proved that he desperately loves you? Husbands, wouldn't you want to do the same?

Raising Children

By extension, as you and your spouse learn to love, teach your children to do the same. The *Shema*, the cornerstone of all of scripture, says that we are to "Love the Lord our God with all our heart and with all our soul and with all our strength" (Deuteronomy 6:5). All the discussions of the Shema I have ever heard end there. What comes next however is of crucial importance. The author says that you are to "Impress them on your children. Talk about them when you sit at home and when you walk along the road, when you lie down and when you get up. Tie them as symbols on your hands and bind them on your foreheads. Write them on the doorframes of your houses and on your gates" (Deuteronomy 6:7-9).

Literally, surround yourself with these commands.

How else would your children know of God and love?

If you think two hours of church programming a week is going to form your children into godly men and women, you are wrong. Those two hours might plant a seed but without nurturing, there will be no growth; they will die with the rest of the world and the world is far too enticing to not support them in finding life in God.

The Israelites were given this task to teach their children what loving God meant. The reason why the Israelites struggled so much throughout the Old Testament was precisely because they failed to raise their children well (Judges 2:10-12). When one generation does not know God, it is very unlikely that their children will.

Unfortunately, our children, like us, are born with original sin. For those of you who are parents, you will know that it begins to take root very early on in life. The early years of your child's life are the years that you need to be most active in shaping and teaching them. There is a Chinese proverb that says, "The first three years determine the next sixty." Essentially, who your child learns to be in his/her first three years will have a drastic impact on who they will become later in life. If you allow their sinful nature to grow deep within them, it will be all that much harder for them to turn it later in life.

Teach your children to love. This is the most important task of a parent. Even when you think they won't understand, what they lack in cognitive ability they make up for in observance. Therefore, it is very important that you not only teach your children to love, but to demonstrate love through the way you live.

Please remember, though, that even if you do it well, it does not promise that your children will not abandon God by their own choices. Your task is to mentor, to guide, to challenge and most importantly, to continue to love them. For even though we, as God's children, continually abandon him, he does not leave us nor forsake us; his love does not depart us in our failure but supports us to stand up again. It is his grace that provides us the strength to turn around.

Submission to authority

Right around the one-year mark of life, we begin to test our authorities. We begin to see what we can get away with. This escalates usually around the second and third years of life as our little wills become more active and demanding. Unfortunately for many, it doesn't stop—ever.

We live in a world where there are clear authority figures in place. Our government has established laws that all people, by living under their authority, are to abide by. Our parents make rules for us in order to keep us safe and to contribute to the family system. Public places, such as shops and parks, have rules to provide the best and safest (and most sanitary) experience for those who come to visit them. If you look closely, you will find that there are rules in our culture everywhere.

Many people think that breaking some of these rules will be of little consequence or that no one will really care, such as speeding, copying coupons, admitting more guests than your gym membership allows, slacking on chores, etc. But if there is a clear authority figure that says to you, "You should not do this" and you continue to do it anyway, what does this tell you about the situation?

It tells me that you think you are above the law, that your way is better and consequently, both the law and the person who made the law (James 4:11-12) are inferior to you. Laws are always attached to people. Your reign is not exerted merely over a piece of paper or a sign, but over a person.

Your sinful nature is still active.

Baptism

"Don't you know that all of us who were baptized into Christ Jesus were baptized into his death? We were therefore buried with him through baptism into death in order that, just as Christ was raised from the dead through the glory of the Father, we too may live a new life" (Romans 6:3-4).

Being immersed in water essentially has two components and both are incredibly symbolic. The first is that we are put under the water which signifies we have died with Christ. The second is that we are raised from the water signifying that we have risen with Christ. This is so much more than a mere action however. It is a public declaration that we have died to our self-reign and have reoriented our lives to Christ and to love. This declaration is not something that should be taken lightly however but it is something to be immensely celebrated for we have become a new humanity!

Communion

On the night Jesus was betrayed, he took the bread, broke it and said, "This is my body given for you; do this in remembrance of me" (Luke 22:19). He then took the cup and said, "This cup is the new covenant in my blood, which is poured out for you" (Luke 22:20). In the mind of the first century Jew, Jesus' words would have reminded them of the time when Abraham made his covenant with God by "breaking" in half a heifer, a goat, a ram and some birds, pouring out their blood and placing them before God.

Thus, symbolically, Jesus was also initiating a covenant ceremony with his disciples. By taking the bread and cup, the disciples were essentially cementing their commitment to following Jesus, saying, "Yes, we will live in the way that you ask."

How does Jesus ask that we live?

"Remember me."

When we typically here the words, "Do this in remembrance of me," we take a piece of bread and some grape juice and briefly remember Jesus. But is this what he really had in mind? The antecedent of "this" is slightly ambiguous. What does it refer to? Considering that a covenant was not a onetime activity but ensured a way of life, the antecedent could not refer to a ritual. I suggest it rather refers to the breaking not of bread or pouring of wine, but the breaking of our bodies and the pouring of our blood. Every act of self sacrifice (i.e. love) should be done in remembrance of Jesus.

Jesus' new covenant is calling his participants to engage radically in love with one another.

And we are to do it in remembrance of him.

Reconciliation

Whenever anyone mentions "reconciliation," people usually think in racial terms. It has become the watchword for racial issues. But reuniting the races is not the definition of reconciliation.

Now, don't get me wrong. Racism is an incredibly heinous offence. But it is the work of the devil to exalt one manifestation of sin over another. We get caught up in our condemning one sin only to turn our backs on so many others. Racism is often highlighted as an atrocious sin, and indeed it is, but often what happens is that while we turn to fight against racism we turn our backs on the fight against gossip, greed, lying, cheating, and envy. Instead of fighting against the sinful *nature,* we focus on a single expression of it.

We compartmentalize our intolerance.

However, only when we engage in the spiritual warfare of fighting against the nature that produces sin can reconciliation truly happen. We must first be reconciled to God through Christ (2 Corinthians 5:18). Realigning our hearts back towards God is reconciliation's primary task. Then, having been reconciled to God, we can take up the task to bring others into a reconciliatory and redemptive state with God (2 Corinthians 5:19).

Worship

The first time "worship" is mentioned in scripture is in Genesis 22. Having finally granted a son to Abraham in his old age, God commands Abraham to sacrifice his son Isaac as a burnt offering. So, the next morning, Abraham got up and prepared his donkey for the journey to the place he would sacrifice Isaac. As they reached the place, Abraham told his servants to "Stay here with the donkey while I and the boy go over there. We will worship and then we will come back to you" (Genesis 22:5).

Abraham fully understood what he was going to do with his son "over there."

He called it "worship."

Abraham's act of obedience in this time of trial was to trust, his act of worship. Obedience to God is the expression of our love for him: "If you love me, you will obey me" (John 14:21).

And what is God's command?

Love one another as I have loved you (John 15:12). Our worship of God is living out of love for him and for one another. Each act of love is the proclamation that only God is worthy of glory, power, honor and praise.

Fasting

Fasting is typically understood as the going without food in order that we might intentionally seek God during that time. We understand that food is necessary for our survival and we therefore cast that off in order to seek he who sustains our life.

This is all well and good.

The problem, however, is that fasting is often ritualistic. Although rituals do remind us of the divine, we tend to think that the it is the rituals that are the greatest expression of our faith, not our lives as a whole. Rituals tend to promote, yet again, compartmentalization of the spiritual vs. the secular.

But God rather asks that our fasting be a way of life:

> Is this the kind of fast I have chosen,
> only a day for a man to humble himself?

> Is it only for bowing one's head like a reed
> and for lying on sackcloth and ashes?
> Is that what you call a fast,
> a day acceptable to the Lord?
> Is not this the kind of fasting I have chosen:
> to lose the chains of injustice
> and untie the cords of the yoke,
> to set the oppressed free
> and break every yoke?
> Is it not to share your food with the hungry
> and to provide the poor wanderer with shelter—
> when you see the naked, to clothe him,
> and not to turn away from your own flesh and blood?
> Then your light will break forth like the dawn,
> and your healing will quickly appear;
> then your righteousness will go before you,
> and the glory of the Lord will be your rear guard (Isaiah 58:4-8).

At its foundation, fasting is the humbling of the self for the acknowledgement of God. That humility is expressed through the way we interact with other people. If we only bow our heads when we are denying food, we essentially deny God all other times.

Fasting is a way of life; not a ritual.

Prayer

There is a prayer I often find myself repeating, tweaking it slightly depending on where I am:

"May Your Kingdom come, may your will be done, on earth as it is in heaven. In my home as it is in heaven. In my school as it is in heaven" (Matthew 6:10).

I find that if I am not intentional, my prayers become very me-focused. What do *I* want? What do *I* need? What situation am *I* going through that needs prayer?

We usually go to God in prayer when we are in need. We hope that somehow the vending machine will produce for us what we desire at that moment. So we provide friends with "prayer requests" (which are still important) but never with "prayer thanks" or "prayer confessions."

But is prayer really about me at all? If I am selfishly praying out of my own reign, who am I praying to? Because if I am praying solely for *my* needs and wants, God is really of no concern to me, only what he can offer me. I must be praying to myself.

What would happen if I began to pray in faith, trust and love for God and others? What if instead I glorified God in prayer as my merciful savior rather than simply either expect something good will happen to me or check this duty off my spiritual to-do list?

I believe lives would be changed.

"If my people, who are called by my name, will humble themselves and pray and seek my face and turn from their wicked ways, then will I hear from heaven and will forgive their sin and will heal their land" (2 Chronicles 7:14).

Sabbath

Sabbath has always been understood within the context of creation. God told his people to observe the Sabbath because on the sixth day of creation, God finished his work and on the seventh day he abstained from work and rested (Exodus 31:17).

What the Jews understood regarding Sabbath, however, was that it was only in part a "day of rest." They understood that Sabbath spoke more towards creation than it did of resting and that resting must be understood within the context of creation.

Sabbath, in other words, was the realization that we are not creators (i.e. God) and therefore should spend time intentionally acknowledging this truth. They therefore "rested" from all things that brought their mind toward creating (working, building, progress) and reflected on who they were as creations before their creator.

When Jesus says that "man was not made for the Sabbath but the Sabbath for man" (Mark 2:27), he was cutting across the assumption of the day that the Sabbath was a legalistic ritual that good Jews adhered to. The implication of legalism however is that a standard is actually attainable and in so "achieving" that standard, people put themselves above others. Legalism is a cornerstone of self-reign.

Sabbath is rather an intentional acknowledgment of who God is and us observing that we are not him.

Its point is to learn humility *through* restoration.

Service

Jesus told his disciples that "I am among you as one who serves" (Luke 22:27). This is clearly evident as he washed their feet (John 13) and made his way to Calvary.

For those of us who are now identified with Jesus, his life, his cross and his resurrection, we too are among humanity as those who serve.

Service is what love looks like when it is given hands and feet.

Mission

"Go and make disciples of all nations, baptizing them in the name of the Father and the Son and the Holy Spirit, and teaching them to obey everything I have commanded you" (Matthew 28:19-20).

The great commission (Matthew 28:16-20) is often quoted before missions trips. And appropriately so. But what we fail to realize is that this text is meant for all disciples of Jesus, not only those who feel "called" to missions work.

We are all called to missions work.

In the vast majority of our English texts, the great commission has two commands: "Go" and "Make disciples." But in the original Greek text, there is only one: "Make disciples." "Go" in the Greek is a participle: it denotes continuing action or something that is done consistently. "In going wherever life takes you, make disciples..."

But it doesn't end there. We are to teach them to obey all that Jesus commands: love God, love one another, and as they follow this command and have died to themselves, baptize them.

Missions are meant for all of us at all times. Our offices are mission fields. Our schools are mission fields. Our ball parks, our homes, our streets, our resorts, our lakes and all places that Christ followers walk are their mission fields.

Evangelism

Someone once asked, "How badly do you have to hate someone to not tell them of salvation?" We hold something of invaluable worth. We would really have to hate someone to keep it to ourselves.

And yet we do every day.

Evangelism begins first by acknowledging the God-given worth of those around you, and second by realizing that they, like you, are in need of a Saviour. If it is true that we are given our worth by God's breath in us, then people should realize their great worth and begin to acknowledge God in our presence.

Like missions, our evangelism is continual because as we direct our lives back toward God in reciprocating love, we become the face, hands and feet of Christ to the world. All our interactions are evangelistic. As St. Francis of Assisi said: "Preach the gospel at all times and if necessary, use words."

Our walk should be our evangelism.

Our face should be the face of Christ.

But if our goal is to put just another notch in our belt, to win the apologetic conversation or to get someone to make a confession of repentance, then we are demonizing our very call to evangelize. We are again making evangelism all about ourselves.

We must first see humanity's worth in the eyes of God, and then instill them with the source of their worth.

It would be wicked not to.

Giving

We often celebrate those who give much, and we should. But who has given more, the person who earns 100 thousand dollars and gives 10 thousand, or the person who earns ten dollars and gives nine?

Giving is not to be done legalistically but generously. However, we often put our three percent (very rarely is it even ten percent, the traditional tithe) in the offering plate and claim that our giving is done for the month. Later in the month, we are hesitant to give to real needs that we see on the street corner or within our community because we feel we have done our duty.

The call of the disciple is to give to whatever extent we are able whenever there is a realized need; and to do it joyfully. "Each man should give what he has decided in his heart to give, not reluctantly or under compulsion, for God loves a cheerful giver" (2 Corinthians 9:7).

After all, nothing is really ours. Everything we have is already a gift generously and graciously provided us from God.

Shouldn't we do the same?

The greater gift is the one given in joy and in generosity. Whether that be a thousand dollars or two pennies is of no concern to God.

But we should ask ourselves if it is loving to give only two pennies to support a need when you have a thousand to give.

Consider this:

As he looked up, Jesus saw the rich putting their gifts into the temple treasury. He also saw a poor widow put in two very small copper coins. "I tell you the truth," he said, "this poor widow has put in more than all the others. All these people gave their gifts out of their wealth; but she out of her poverty put in all she had to live on (Luke 21:1-4).

We are called to give at all times in whatever extent we are able.

And to do so joyfully.

The Kingdom of God, realized in agape love and God's reign, is the most prized of possessions. There is nothing in this world that can compare to its worth (Matthew 13:44).

But do we believe it?

I wonder how our lives would change if we did?

endnotes

[i] See www.reviewjournal.com/lvrj_home/2005/May-28-Sat-2005/news/26616663.html

[ii] See www.ryanpatrickhalligan.org

[iii] C.S. Lewis, *A Grief Observed* (New York: HarperSanFrancisco, 1961), 46.

[iv] Dietrich Bonhoeffer, *The Cost of Discipleship* (New York: Touchstone, 1959), 43.

[v] C.S. Lewis, *The Pilgrims Regress* (Grand Rapids: Wm. B. Eerdmans Publishing Co., 1933), 5.

[vi] C.S. Lewis, *Mere Christianity* (New York: HarperSanFrancisco, 1952), 49.

[vii] C.S. Lewis, *God in the Dock* (Grand Rapids: Wm. B. Eerdmans Publishing Co., 1970), 112.

[viii] C.S. Lewis, *The Weight of Glory* (New York: HarperSanFrancisco, 1949), 25.

[ix] See http://www.pewterreport.com/forum/index.php?PHPSESSID=c9e3e975514e049dd5882159c5b2d9bf&action=printpage;topic=31767.0

[x] Soren Kierkegaard, *Provocations* (Maryknoll, New York: Orbis Books, 2002), 11.

[xi] See http://investors.bonton.com/releasedetail.cfm?releaseid=347074

[xii] See http://www.brandsoftheworld.com/catalogue/J/118746.html

[xiii] See http://www.prnewswire.com/cgi-bin/micro_stories.pl?ACCT=116376&TICK=SEARS&STORY=/www/story/08-17-1999/0001005029&EDATE=Aug+17,+1999

[xiv] See http://findarticles.com/p/articles/mi_m0FNP/is_10_41/ai_86204687/

[xv] See http://www.dealerscope.com/article/best-buys-holiday-advertising-uses-slogan-you-happier-400682_1.html

[xvi] See http://www.vincenthorn.com/2007/01/13/happiness-is-just-a-curly-fry-away/

[xvii] See www.savemoneylivebetter.com

[xviii] C.S. Lewis, *The Great Divorce* (New York: Harperone, 1946), 75.

[xix] C.S. Lewis, *The Problem of Pain* (New York: HarperSanFrancisco, 1940), 91.

[xx] John Donne, "Meditation XVII" from *Devotions Upon Urgent Occasions*, 108-109.

[xxi] Abraham Cohen, *Everyman's Talmud* (New York: Shocken Books, 1949), 184.

[xxii] C.S. Lewis, *The Srewtape Letters* (New York: HarperSanFrancisco, 1942), 155.

[xxiii] Bonhoeffer, *The Cost of Discipleship*, 43

[xxiv] Lewis, *The Great Divorce*, title page

[xxv] See http://www.numenware.com/article/268

[xxvi] See http://askville.amazon.com/decisions-day-average-person make/AnswerViewer.do?requestId=16336722

[xxvii] See http://wiki.answers.com/Q/How_many_words_a_person_speaks_in_a_day

[xxviii] Lewis, *The Screwtape Letters*, 155

Made in the USA